A WEE GUIDE TO
Robert Burns

A WEE GUIDE TO

Robert Burns

Dilys Jones

GOBLINSHEAD

Musselburgh

A WEE GUIDE TO Robert Burns

First Published 1997
Reprinted 1998, 2002, 2005 (with updating),
2008 (reset with updating)
© Martin Coventry 1997, 2005, 2008
Text © Dilys Jones & Martin Coventry 1997
Published by GOBLINSHEAD
130B Inveresk Road
Musselburgh EH21 7AY Scotland
tel 0131 665 2894
email goblinshead@sol.co.uk

Dedication
Dedicated to Anne Banister. The next one's yours –

British Library Cataloguing in Publication Data
A catalogue record for this book is available from the
British Library.

ISBN 978 1 899874 07 1

Typeset by GOBLINSHEAD using Desktop Publishing

Wee Guides
• **Scottish History**
• **Prehistoric Scotland** • **The Picts**
• **St Margaret and Malcolm Canmore**
• **William Wallace** • **Robert the Bruce**
• **Mary, Queen of Scots**
• **The Jacobites** • **Rob Roy MacGregor** • **Flora MacDonald**
• **Robert Burns** • **Whisky**
• **Scottish Ghosts and Bogles**

Look Out for Goblinshead's Thistle Guide series

A WEE GUIDE TO
Robert Burns

Contents

List of Illustrations

Acknowledgements

I'm indebted to Laurence Hunter for very many things, but as far as this book is concerned, I need to thank him for the loan of *The Central Episode*, an excellent monograph written by his father, the late Walter Kerr Hunter of Kirkcudbright, and expanded by Ian Campbell. I have used this extensively as a source in Chapter 3 and elsewhere, and am grateful to Laurence and to Mrs Elizabeth Hunter for the opportunity to do so. The insights in that chapter are all Mr Hunter's; the deficiencies mine.

Dr David Johnson of Napier University was very generous with his time and his insights into Burns the song-writer, to which the scope of this book cannot do justice.

Last but not least, a big thank you to Joyce Miller and Martin Coventry of Goblinshead for support, encouragement and liquid refreshment.

Illustrations

Many thanks to the following for their kind permission to use illustrations:

Alexander Naysmith: Robert Burns (*cover*) & Archibald Skirving: Robert Burns (*frontispiece* & page 47) The Scottish National Portrait Gallery.

Jean Armour – reproduced from Wilson & Chambers: The Land of Burns. Glasgow, 1840 (page 22), Burns' funeral procession, Dumfries, 25 July 1796 – reproduced from engraving NLS MSS.15966 (page 48), 'The Carlin caught her by the rump ...' illustration from Tam o' Shanter – Burns: The Illustrated Family Burns. 1879 (page 60), & The Cotter's Saturday Night – reproduced from The Cotter's Saturday Night. 1853 (page 73) The Trustees of the National Library of Scotland.

Bachelors' Club (page 15), Clay figures – Souter Johnnie's Cottage (page 74), Souter Johnnie's Cottage (page 82) National Trust for Scotland.

Photographs by Dilys Jones

How to Use this Book

This book is divided into three parts:

- Part One (pages 5–48) describes Burns' life and the events surrounding him, with maps (page 4 & 12), and a Calendar of events (page 2).

- Part Two (pages 49-77) contains many of Burns' best-known or loved poems – *Scots Wha Hae* (page 49); *Address to a Haggis* (page 50); *Red, Red Rose* (page 52); *Auld Lang Syne* (page 53); *Tam o' Shanter* (page 54); and *Ae Fond Kiss* (page 61) – and includes a discussion of his work in chapter 8 (page 62).

- Part Three consists of places, associated with the life and times of Burns, to visit (pages 79-83) listing over 25 attractions. Information includes access, opening days, facilities and a brief description; and a map locates all the sites (page 78).

A glossary (pages 84-5) includes Scots words used in Burns' poems, and an index (pages 86-7) lists all the main people and events.

Warning

While the information in this book was believed to be correct at time of going to press – and was checked, where possible, with the visitor attractions – opening times and facilities, or other information, may vary or differ from that included. All information should be checked with the visitor attractions before embarking on any journey. Inclusion in the text is no indication whatsoever that a site is open to the public or that it should be visited. The publisher and author cannot accept responsibility for damage or injury caused from any visit.

The places listed to visit are only a personal selection of what is available, and the inclusion or exclusion of a visitor attraction in the text should not be considered as a comment or judgement on that attraction.

Locations on maps may be approximate.

Introduction

In the Snug Bar of the Globe Inn, Dumfries – a place warmly recommended to any traveller – an elderly gentleman, whose name I never knew, spoke eloquently of Scotland's national bard. He spoke as if of a close friend recently lost, and closed his comments with the remark: 'Ye canna blame genius for anything'.

What is most striking about the reputation of Robert Burns, 200 years after his death, is precisely this personal regard in which the man is held. Walk into an English pub and ask people there what they think of William Shakespeare or T S Eliot and the response – at best – is likely to be an indifferent shrug: it is hard to think of any other poet with such a human face.

In Scotland, even people who don't much like poetry and never read it anyway have an opinion on Burns. Burns gave the common man a voice, and that voice rings out loud and clear today. From Canada to Japan, from Moscow to Johannesburg, his character is as genuinely admired as his poetry – and sometimes more so. This short book attempts to tell the remarkable story of his life and the events that shaped that character.

DJ, Edinburgh, 1997

Calendar of Events

1745-6   The Jacobite Uprising attempts to restore a Stewart king to the British throne

1748   The Burnes (or Burness) family leave Kincardineshire – William to Edinburgh

1757   William Burnes marries Agnes Brown of Kirkoswald

1759   Robert Burns born in Alloway, 25 January

1760   Birth of Robert's brother Gilbert: other children follow

1766   The Burnes family move to Mount Oliphant, near Alloway

1776   The American War of Independence begins. The Burns family move to Lochlie farm

1781   Robert Burns becomes a Freemason. Burns moves to Irvine to learn the trade of flax-dressing

1784   Death of William Burnes. Robert moves his family to Mossgiel and changes the spelling of the family name to Burns; probably meets Jean Armour in this year

1785   Burns completes many of the poems for the Kilmarnock edition including *The Cotter's Saturday Night*

1786   The Kilmarnock edition of Burns' poems is published; Jean Armour gives birth to twins; death of Highland Mary; Burns goes to Edinburgh

1787   First Edinburgh edition of poems published by William Creech; first volume of the *Scots Musical Museum* (edited by Burns) published – five more follow

1788   Burns returns to Dumfriesshire and takes lease on Ellisland; marries Jean Armour

1789   Storming of the Bastille and the start of the French Revolution; Burns becomes an Exciseman

1791   Burns gives up Ellisland and moves his family to Dumfries (11 Bank Street)

1792   Burns promoted to Dumfries Port Division; on 29 February the smuggling ship *Rosamond* is seized

1793   The Burns family move to Mill Vennel, now 24 Burns Street; The Second Edinburgh edition of his poems published by William Creech – this includes *Tam o' Shanter*; Thomas Muir of Huntershill is sentenced to 14 years' transportation; King Louis XVI and Queen Marie Antoinette are executed in France

1794   Burns promoted to Supervisor; re-issue of the Second Edinburgh edition

1795   Burns joins the Royal Dumfries Volunteers; in September his daughter Elizabeth dies and Burns becomes gravely ill with rheumatic fever

1796   Meal Riots in Dumfries; Burns continues to work until June in rapidly deteriorating health; on 3 July goes to Brow on Solway on medical advice but fails to revive; dies in Dumfries on 21 July

1817   On the night of 19 September, Burns' remains moved to the Mausoleum in St Michael's Kirkyard from their original resting-place

1834   Death of Jean Armour, who is buried beside Burns in his Mausoleum

Map 1: Burns' Scotland

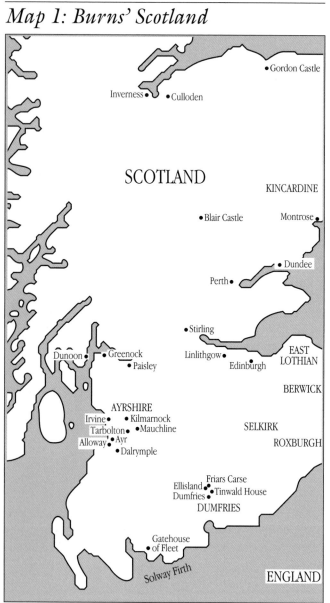

1 – *The Land and the City*

The brief life of Robert Burns was but a handspan in the second half of the eighteenth century. He died before he was 40 years old, his health broken by the hard physical labour of a boyhood spent doing a man's work on his father's farm. Yet in those years Burns not only witnessed great revolutions abroad – in America in 1776, in France in 1789 – but lived through a revolution at home in every way as turbulent.

This revolution had its roots, quite literally, in the land: who owned it and how, what it yielded, and how much, and by what means. Burns was born into a Scotland still farmed as a peasant culture: the laird (or landowner) owned the land outright, and his tenants farmed it for his benefit and the benefit of his heirs. In return for a lifetime of loyalty and hard work, they could take what they needed for their families: a roof over their heads, and enough land to cultivate food to put in their children's mouths. It was a life lived on the edge of enough: any surplus must of right belong to the landowner; any less – the result, for example, of a bad harvest or pestilence among animals – and the family would fall through the fragile net of sufficiency into the pit of poverty which lay unforgivingly beneath.

When Burns was born, the land was not fenced or walled. Visitors who look at the neat parcelled fields of Ayrshire today are looking at an order created during Burns' lifetime – as a boy, he would have looked upon unfettered open space where it was accepted that land was owned by one but used by all: in fact, a commonwealth of rough grazing. Each man took from it what he needed: peat or timber for fuel, grazing for his animals, and a patch of soil round his cottage for food.

The revolution that transformed the countryside of lowland Scotland from open muir – or meadow – to enclosed farmland came about as the old order creaked and collapsed under the burdens of the new: the population explosion which began during the eighteenth century meant more babies certain to survive into adulthood, more mouths demanding more food, larger towns and cities hungry for produce, and an agricultural hinterland which needed to move, almost overnight, from peasant economy to an efficient producer of abundant surplus. With the urgent need to improve the quality of land came the need for lime, and lime needed transportation: the Turnpike Acts of 1766 and 1774 began the irrevocable process of transforming rough bridlepath into major highway down which crime and disorder could travel as fast as food and culture.

The Scotland into which Burns was born was essentially two cultures in one nation: Highland and Lowland. It has been observed that the citizens of Edinburgh and the market-minded Lowlander felt more in common even with the English than with the Highland society and culture of fact and legend.

The Battle of Culloden, that Hanoverian killing spree which placed a bloody fullstop on the Jacobite uprising of 1745-6, was well within living memory and that memory a bitter one. The Highlander became a hunted creature: what the sword and the fire of Hanoverian armies failed to do in 1746, subsequent years of harsh legislation achieved. Some Highlanders had already taken ship for the New World or for Australia. The 1707 Act of Union between the parliaments of England and Scotland came to be seen for what it was: the suffocation of the Scots identity by a heavy-handed government hundreds of miles away in London.

The capital city, Edinburgh, where Burns lived for two years, was consolidating its reputation as the Athens of the North. For hundreds of years, the city had huddled in diseased and insanitary squalor around and below the castle walls. Rich and poor lived side by side – or more accurately, on top of one another in high tenements, some of them 14 storeys – called

Gladstone's Land – a 17th-century Edinburgh tenement

'lands'. Into every available inch of space they crowded, the class structure made manifest by the floor you inhabited: clerks and menial workers on the lower levels, the wealthy in the middle, the merchants just above them with a few more stairs to climb – those middle classes thus forming a buffer between the rich and the poor, who lived under the stars at the very top. The smell was overpowering: toilet slops were ritually emptied from the windows at 10pm, and it was remarked that Edinburgh by night was 'perilous underfoot'.

By 1772, however, the great exodus of the rich across the Red Sea of Princes Street had be-gun. George Street and Queen Street were under develop-ment and graceful buildings reached to-wards the village of Stockbridge. From their plum-red, rose-pink, or sea-green drawing-rooms in the New Town, adorned with fireplaces by Adam and furniture by Chippendale, the rich could look up at the castle against the sky-line, and reflect on the real distance they had travelled. Lawyers, bankers, merchants, physicians and intel-lectuals, the pride of

Georgian House – part of the elegant New Town

Edinburgh society rested on the right choice of school, of profession and of church. Adam Smith wrote *The Wealth of Nations* here: but Edinburgh could still claim a variety and richness of life. In the bawdy taverns of the Grassmarket business was thriving, and when Burns was in Edinburgh, the colourful saga of Deacon Brodie was drawing to a close.

William Brodie – inspiration a century later for *Dr Jekyll and Mr Hyde*

– was by day a respected city councillor and pillar of society; by night, a thief and a gambler with loaded dice. Brodie was caught and hanged on 1 October 1788 from the city's new 'humane' drop-gallows – gallows which ironically he himself had commissioned as being more merciful than the older custom of turning victims off a ladder. In one of his very worst poems, Burns saluted Edinburgh as

Edina! Scotia's darling seat ...

(It must be noted that many years later one of the first manufacturers of toilet bowls used the trade-name Edina for their product. This seems fittingly ironic in view of Edinburgh's previous reputation as an open sewer.)

South of Edinburgh and Glasgow, the Lowland counties prospered by farming. A man might pursue another trade such as shoe-making or inn-keeping, but there was often a farm to tend as well. Farming and the land were absolutely interwoven into the fabric of everyday life. Even so, the eighteenth-century Lowland Scot had a level of education that was second to none, and literacy levels were impressively high. The Education Acts of 1649 and 1696 required each parish to provide a school.

Society loves to hang labels on people – and all too often hang them by their labels. When Robert Burns rode to Edinburgh in 1786, hot with the success of his first published verse, elegant society lionised him as 'the Ploughman Poet'. They loved the – patronising – idea of a rough, scarcely educated boy, ignorant of the manners of the drawing-room, the dinner table or the lady's boudoir, shivering in the mud behind his plough in Ayrshire and plucking warm verse from the frozen air.

Burns used this image as far as it was to his advantage but was quick to see through the falsity of the society which created it. His genius may have been a gift from the gods, but he cultivated it as assiduously as he cultivated the stony, meagre earth he farmed. He was by no means uneducated – a veneration for education is an integral part of Scots culture, and Burns' father contrived for his sons as solid an education as was possible. Burns at 13 – the age by which any formal education had ceased – was arguably better (and more enthusiastically) educated than many an upper-class counterpart in expensive private schooling.

In the drawing rooms of the rich he conducted himself with an ease and a steady gaze that some found offensive. And he spent only two years in what he called 'the noise and nonsense' of Edinburgh before returning to where he felt most himself – the land.

In the best of his poetry, Robert Burns used the Scots language to record and to honour this unique heritage: he expressed and embodied the very contradictions of his native country – blood and sophistication, murder and magic, roughness and civility. The hand that steadied a plough also scratched lines of verse on glass – with a diamond.

2 – His Father's Son 1759-84

My father was a farmer upon the Carrick border, O;
And carefully he bred me in decency and order, O;
He bade me act a manly part, though I had ne'er a farthing, O;
For without an honest manly heart, no man was worth regarding, O.

The spelling of the family name had been Burnes or Burness, and they came from the north of Scotland, from Kincardineshire, where the poet's grandfather and namesake, Robert Burnes, had been a gardener at Inverugie Castle. They rented land directly from the Earl Marischal, and were thus comfortable farming people, with status in their local community.

The story runs that the family were sympathetic to the Jacobite cause enshrined in Bonnie Prince Charlie and the uprising of 1745. Given their Highland roots this would not be surprising, and Robert Burns himself had in adult life a romantic attachment to the Stewart cause.

Whatever their true sympathies, the Burnes family suffered economically as a direct consequence of the uprising and the punitive measures taken against the Highlands by the London government. William Burnes, the elder Robert's son, had been born in 1721, the youngest of three sons. In 1748 the family went their separate ways in order, simply, to survive – one son to Montrose, one to Ayrshire, and William to Edinburgh, where he found work as a landscape gardener.

William's description of the pain he felt at parting from his brothers, each facing an unknown future, made a great impression on his sons. His second son Gilbert later wrote: 'I have often heard my father describe the anguish of mind he felt when he parted with his elder brother Robert on the top of a hill ... each going off his several way in search of new adventures, and scarcely knowing whither he went.'

For two years William worked in the capital – for some time in that part where a loch had been drained and known as The Meadows. But in 1750 he moved west, to Ayrshire, with ambitions to restore his family's fortunes as tenant farmers. For a while, he was gardener to Alexander Fairlie, an Ayrshire laird. This was no unimportant post, for the gardens of a great house not only testified to a man's position by their beauty and the modernity of their landscaping – gardening being the 'new' art form of the eighteenth century – but in practical terms put fruit and vegetables on a man's table to feed his family and his guests.

But William Burnes moved on – he acquired seven and a half acres at Alloway and set up as a nurseryman himself, although as this alone was insufficient to support a family, he also worked as head gardener at Doonside, a private estate. On 15 December 1757 William married Agnes Brown, a farmer's daughter from Kirkoswald whom he may have met at Maybole Fair in 1756. Agnes had pale red hair and a temper to match, though a cheerful disposition, and was a capable farm-bred woman: the eldest of six and motherless from the age of ten, she had looked after her younger siblings when their mother died.

To house his wife and family, William built a house on that seven and a half acres with his own hands. This was a traditional but-and-ben, the 'auld cley biggin' Burns described, a simple dwelling with a clay floor and a peat-burning fire. Box-beds might have a concealing curtain, but life in such cottages was a public affair. Children slept with their parents, though the boys might sleep with the animals in the byre. There might be one chair for the patriarch of the family, one cooking pot and a lamp above the fire. In the long winter evenings, a lull in song or conversation would be punctuated by the snufflings and shufflings of the animals behind the dividing wall.

The first child of William and Agnes was born on 25 January 1759 and

Burns Cottage, Alloway – Robert was born here 25 January 1759

named Robert for his grandfather. When Robert was a few days old, a violent storm blew up and the gable end of the cottage collapsed. Mother and baby took shelter with a neighbour until the damage was repaired.

Six more children were to follow over the years: Gilbert – to whom

Robert was very close in affection as well as age – Agnes, Annabella, William, John and the last, Isabella, in 1771. Describing that clay but-and-ben, John Murdoch, tutor to the elder boys, wrote: 'In this cottage ... I really believe there dwelt a larger portion of content than in any Palace in Europe. [Burns' poem] *The Cotter's Saturday Night* will give some idea of the temper and manners that prevailed there.'

The cottage was soon overflowing with children, and in 1765 William Burnes took a 12-year lease on a farm at Mount Oliphant, two miles from Alloway. Burnes was required to make a huge capital investment to stock the farm – a sum over twice the annual rental. Both at Mount Oliphant and later at Lochlie – the farm in Tarbolton parish to which he moved in 1777 – William's story, and that of his family, has the same tragic theme: back-breaking and relentless physical toil, the gradual erosion of whatever meagre savings or capital might have been saved, debts and disappointments mounting with each poor harvest, each harsh winter, every unrewarding spring.

In his poems and songs, Robert Burns reveals an acute understanding of the farmer's life with its utter dependence on the soil, the seasons and the beasts. He did not learn this sympathy, but saw it lived, in his father, his brothers and himself.

Agnes churned the butter, made the cheese and minded the children with a fierce and loving eye. She also, not incidentally, possessed an ear for music and a fine singing voice – two attributes her eldest son always found irresistible in a woman.

William Burnes was a Calvinist and a stern, uncompromising up-holder of that dry morality against which Robert would later rail. The only letter in existence from Robert to his fa-

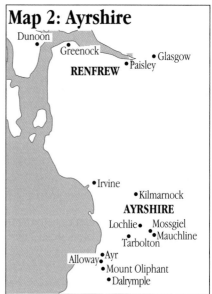

Map 2: Ayrshire

Dunoon

Greenock

Glasgow

RENFREW   Paisley

Irvine

Kilmarnock

AYRSHIRE

Lochlie   Mossgiel

Tarbolton   Mauchline

Alloway   Ayr

Mount Oliphant

Dalrymple

ther begins 'Honoured Sir' which may speak more of respect than love. William found much to exasperate and appal him in a son who so relished such pastimes as dancing and music, yet clearly the bond between the two was close. Robert described his father as 'the best of friends and the ablest of instructors', and William is the inspiration for the *douce guidman* or gentle patriarch of *The Cotter's Saturday Night.* At the Burns Birthplace Museum a printed copy of William's *Manual of Religious Belief* may be seen, a book he wrote in longhand for the moral instruction of his children.

The greatest gift William gave his sons was their education. Life at Mount Oliphant was hard and the family might not see meat on the table from one year to the next, but William placed a value on education that was worth every sacrifice.

When Robert was six, William engaged one John Murdoch to teach his own sons and those of certain neighbours. Murdoch was 18 at the time, and described William Burnes as 'by far the best of the human race that he ever knew'. Murdoch liked the Burnes boys, though it was the cheerful and good-natured Gilbert that was his favourite, and he enjoyed his visits to the cottage he called the 'mud edifice'. The teaching took place in Alloway – a walk of two miles each way, one uphill, one down.

The boys learned to read, to write a little, and mastered the rudiments of grammar. Robert, not surprisingly, became an enthusiastic reader – *The Life of Hannibal* was an early and treasured favourite. Long passages from the Bible and Shakespeare were learnt by heart. This, however, was Murdoch's verdict on the boy whose adult life was passed in the creation and embellishment of Scottish songs: '[His] ear was remarkably dull, and his voice untunable'.

It is worth noting Burns' fluency from boyhood in both his native Scots and in the version of English spoken in Edinburgh drawing-rooms, as well as south of the Border. He was easy with both, as his vast output of letters in either tongue shows – over 700 exist today – and never devalued Scots as being in any way inferior, even when his Edinburgh patron Henry Mackenzie suggested that his poems might have wider appeal if they were written in English.

The three years of formal education in Mr Murdoch's schoolroom ended when Robert was nine, and were the longest sustained period of education in his life. The money could scarce be found and besides, the boy was big enough to take on a job of work on the farm: threshing the grain, and weeding. Later he would walk behind the plough.

His education thereafter was erratic, a matter of weeks here and there spared from farm work. Whenever books or visitors from beyond the confines of the farm came his way, Robert clung to them hungrily. One glorious summer he was sent to Ayr for two weeks, to some relations of his mother's, where he was allowed to use the library and saw, for the first time, rows upon rows of books, all waiting to be read. John Murdoch was by this time a Master at Ayr Academy, and Robert studied again with him. He did in fact learn a little Latin, though in later life he declared that the only Latin of which he had need was *omnia vincit amor* – love conquers all.

In 1772 William Burnes sent Robert and Gilbert to a school in Dalrymple for a few weeks – in a building now the White Horse Hotel – in order that their handwriting might be improved. While here, Robert read a book about William Wallace, the thirteenth-century Scot who became a particular hero to the boy.

As he grew into a young man, the sense of frustration within Robert became more apparent. He is described in these years as touchy, proud and sure of himself. A boy doing a man's work, he must have yearned for the world of books, of conversation, of education, that was so tantalisingly beyond his reach. He knew himself to be intelligent and able – but the circumstances of his life required him to weed the furrows before the plough, and tend to animals when he would so much rather tend to the world of imagination and ideas instead. His brother Gilbert noted in him a tendency to envy others: 'Robert cherished a particular jealousy of people who were richer or of more consequence than himself.' The lines he wrote in *Man was Made to Mourn* have a particular 'eloquence':

If I'm designed yon lordling's slave,
By Nature's law designed,
Why was an independent wish
E'er planted in my mind?

In 1777, when Robert was 18, his father freed himself from the exhausting burden of Mount Oliphant and the family moved to Lochlie, which lies between Tarbolton and Mauchline. William now paid his two sons a man's wage as ploughmen: £7 a year.

The nearby town of Tarbolton provided Robert with new excitements. He was still reading books whenever he could find them, and at Tarbolton first read a novel, popular at the time, which became his lodestar: *The Man of Feeling*. It was 'a book I prize next to the Bible', Burns told Mackenzie later, when the two men became friends in Edinburgh. The book is now unreadable, but it was big on 'sensibility' – that vague quality of emotional delicacy which a young poet would find inspiring.

In Tarbolton, in 1780, Robert and Gilbert founded a debating society which they called the Bachelors' Club. Apart from the obvious qualification, candidates for membership were required to have 'a frank, honest, open

Bachelors' Club, Tarbolton

heart; above anything dirty or mean; and must be a professed lover of one or more of the female sex'. This last was probably more wishful thinking on Robert's part than anything else: his thoughts were increasingly occupied with the delights of courtship and the confusions of lust, even though his efforts in that direction had as yet been unlucky.

His courtship of one Alison Begbie – 'a belle-fille whom I adored' – was conducted by letter and he seems to have wanted to marry her. The facts of this ponderous courtship have been debated by Burns scholars, but the letter proposing marriage is hardly prose to melt the heart:

'If you will be so good and so generous as to admit me for your partner ... there is nothing on this side of eternity shall give me greater transport.'

Whatever the truth, Alison rejected him, chose another, and Burns claimed to have been mortified by the experience. Some even believe this early failure to marry a local lass of good standing and thus replicate his parents' marriage is a key to his later development.

Tarbolton was also the place where Robert attended a dancing class 'to give my manners a brush'. His father was utterly opposed to his attendance, but Robert went anyway.

A lifelong friend, Davie Sillar, describes Burns as already appearing very different from other people: 'His social disposition easily procured him acquaintance; but a certain satirical seasoning ... while it set the rustic circle in a roar, was not unaccompanied by its kindred attendant – suspicious fear ... He wore the only tied hair in the parish...and in the church, his plaid, which was of a particular colour [black and white] ... he wrapped in a particular manner round his shoulders.'

His appetite for life beyond the farm was confirmed by an important event in his life: in 1781 Robert became a Freemason, initiated on 4 July in Lodge No. 174, St David's. Freemasonry was then at the height of its popularity and was a sure route to social acceptability. The author of Burns' favourite book, Henry Mackenzie, was also a mason and one of a distinguished and influential group of masons who welcomed Burns to Edinburgh in 1786 and guaranteed the young poet an entree into all the best circles of society. It was through masonic contacts, as much as his poetry, that Burns was able to mix freely with the rich and the titled.

The romantic ritual of Freemasonry, with its roots in myth and antiquity, satisfied Burns' need for colour and magic in life. More than this, however, eighteenth-century Freemasonry applied the principles of international brotherhood, of fraternal loyalties which transcended class and creed. This 'brotherhood of man' was a concept which grew in importance and value in Burns' life and found ultimate expression in his passionate support for the egalitarian philosophies behind the American and the French Revolutions.

Leisure to indulge in revolutionary fervour was limited, however, by the continuing struggle to make ends meet. As a later poet noted, a different address may only land you in a different kind of mess, and this was certainly true of the move to Lochlie.

The previous chapter described the eighteenth-century revolution in agriculture: this wrench from old to new was achieved by men like William and Robert. The containment of open heathland involves the building of walls, of drains, of ditches – when the old gives way to the new there is immense work to be done in installing the new, but the daily work must go on nevertheless.

In Robert's case, building a wall or draining a field still meant the animals had to be fed and the fields ploughed. He wrote tellingly to a cousin: 'Our landholders, full of ideas of farming gathered from the English and the Lothian and other soil in Scotland, make no allowance for the odds of the quality of the land, and consequently stretch us much beyond in the event, we will be found able to pay.'

What might have worked on fertile, robust soil, withered and died in the sour, stony earth of Lochlie. What is remarkable, though, is that what was flourishing in these years of hardship was the spirit of poetry within Robert Burns. Grabbing at passing morsels of education where they could be found, spending long hours on the land in the hardest of physical work, his eye and his heart remained alive to beauty and to music, finding them equally in pretty girls, in the natural world around him, and in the companionship of friends. No one can be certain exactly when he began to write verse, but one can be certain that the spirit of poetry was thriving as surely as the crops were withering at Lochlie.

In 1781 the 22-year-old Robert went to Irvine, an Ayrshire town made a royal burgh by Robert the Bruce, to learn the trade of flax-combing. At Lochlie, the Burnses had been growing flax as an additional crop, and it was in the interests of expanding the family business that Robert apprenticed himself to one Mr Peacock, flax-dresser or 'heckler'. Rob stayed for six miserable months, during the course of which he was very ill with pleurisy.

But in Irvine there was a bookshop – Templeton's – and Robert spent a great deal of time there, impressed to learn that a poet called Robert Fergusson had earned as much as £50 from publishing a book called *Scots Poems*. The fate of that young and tragic poet moved Burns – Fergusson had died mad and penniless in 1774. Robert Burns freely acknowledged the influence of Fergusson on his own work and in 1787 paid for the erection of a tombstone over his unmarked grave in Edinburgh's Canongate churchyard.

At Irvine Rob made a friend, Richard Brown, a seaman. Burns wrote: 'His knowledge of the world was vastly superior to mine, and I was all attention to learn. He added: He was the only man I ever saw who was a greater fool than myself when woman was the presiding star...'

It was to Brown, one Sunday in Eglinton woods, that Burns repeated some of his verses. Brown was impressed, and suggested that Burns send some of his poems to a magazine: 'and that,' wrote Burns, 'encouraged me to endeavour at the character of a Poet.'

In Irvine, Burns tasted the 'new drink' lately come from the Highlands – whisky. He lost all his possessions in a fire and he lost his virginity too – presumably in a fire of another kind. But the flax-dressing venture failed, and he was needed at home where William Burnes was facing legal action for arrears of rent.

In January 1784 Burns was 25 years old: he had 12 years of life left to him, and the long years of farm work had almost certainly weakened his health in a way that would kill him. Apart from the six months at Irvine, he had lived his life under his father's roof, abiding by his father's principles, under the shadow of his father's misfortune.

Then everything changed. Broken by anxiety and ill luck, William Burnes had been ailing for months. Appealing against the sequestration of Lochlie for arrears of rent had cost him literally the last he had.

On the morning of the 13 February, Robert and his sister Isabella were distressed to find the poisoned body of Rob's dog Luath outside their door – the act of a vengeful neighbour. It must have seemed a sombre omen. With his children gathered round his bed, William said: 'There is only one of you I am afraid for'. His eyes were on Robert. By evening, the father was dead.

Robert was now head of the family, and his own life could begin.

Grave of William Burnes and Agnes Brown – Alloway Kirk

3 – *The Ploughman Poet 1784-6*

> O leave novéls, ye Mauchline belles
> Ye're safer at your spinning-wheel;
> Such witching books are baited hooks
> For rakish rooks like Rob Mossgiel.

A few weeks after his father's death, Robert and his brother Gilbert took over the lease of a 100-acre farm called Mossgiel in Mauchline parish. The rent was £90 a year and Robert was full of enthusiasm for the new venture – 'I read farming books; I calculated crops; I attended markets....' There was a three-roomed cottage for the family, and the young householder was known locally as Rob Mossgiel.

Symbolic of his new life was a subtle change of name, for it is from the time of his father's death that Rob formally changed the spelling of his name from Burnes to Burns. All his life, he loved the capacity to invent and re-invent himself through words.

Other changes became apparent. Free from his father's restraining influence, Robert's relationships with women rapidly became the tangled web they would remain for the rest of his life. A local girl, Lizzie Paton, was pregnant by him and Rob had no intention whatsoever of marrying her – fortunately for him, his brother Gilbert also felt that Lizzie was no suitable match for a Burns.

Lizzie Paton's child was brought up in the Burns household. A characteristic of Burns – by no means usual in those days, or now – which does him credit was his willingness not only to acknowledge his various illegitimate children and accept financial responsibility for them, but an apparent preference for taking these children into his own home. Of his 14 acknowledged children, only five were actually born in wedlock.

Lizzie left the scene and Rob wrote a poem *Welcome to his Bastard Wean* – clearly a fully-fledged artist already in his ability to use personal experience for public entertainment. The poem is usually published under the more genteel title of *A Poet's Welcome to his Love-Begotten Daughter* and it gives a wry insight into the man:

> Tho' now they ca' me fornicator
> An' tease my name in countra clatter
> The mair they talk, I'm kend the better,
> E'en let them clash;

> An auld wife's tongue's a' feckless matter
> To gie ane fash.

Contempt for village chatter does not disguise a certain braggadocio concerning his own sexual prowess, and this is surely tongue-in-cheek:

> Lord grant that thou may aye inherit
> Thy mither's person, grace, an' merit,
> An thy poor, worthless daddy's spirit
> Without his failins ...

But for all the public grief this birth may have given him, there is no hint of it in what is overwhelmingly a poem of proud paternity:

> Welcome! my bonie, sweet, wee dochter
> Tho' ye come here a wee unsought for
> And tho' your comin' I hae fought for
> Baith kirk and queir;
> Yet by my faith ye're no unwrought for,
> That I shall swear!
>
> Sweet fruit o' monie a merry dint,
> My funny toil is no a'tint,
> Tho' thou cam to the warl' asklent,
> Which fools may scoff at;
> In my last plack thy part's be in't
> The better ha'f o't.

The urge to write was powerful and Rob was doing more and more of it – with some guilt. He was a farmer, and had every intention of being a successful one. Verse-making was a distraction from the real business of life – but he had to do it. He carried pen and paper with him everywhere, and the collection of poems, shoved into a drawer in an upstairs room, started to grow. His brother Gilbert noted that holding the plough was a favourite situation with Robert for poetic composition.

For recreation, in nearby Mauchline, there was *Poosie Nansie's* – an establishment as racy as its name suggests and the setting of *The Jolly Beggars*. In this and other taverns, Burns observed, noted, scribbled – and enjoyed. 'Freedom and whisky gang together', he once wrote. His passion was for the fellowship of drink – he loved its companionate nature, the jollity, the stimulation. He was usually a moderate drinker – his weak stomach and poor health saw to that – and seldom arrived at the maudlin, sorrows-drowning edge of drink, although there are recorded episodes when he and his companions became what he referred to as bitchified. His biographer Catherine Carswell notes that Burns was 'never too drunk to write a letter'.

He was now also free to indulge his love of song. His own singing talents may have been minimal – though he was a fiddle player – but he had a superb ear. He only had to hear a ballad once to have its tune and its lyrics imprinted on his memory. For the rest of his life, Rob was to see himself as a 'mender' of old songs as well as a composer of new ones. Scotland's rich heritage of folk song was threatened with disappearance: as people moved to cities and tastes changed, as poverty-stricken Scots fled to the New World, as the kirk maintained its implacable disapproval of song and dance – regarding mixed dancing between men and women as promiscuous – the old songs sung by the fire and in the fields were fading from memory. Burns set himself the task of recording as much as he could, and mending these old songs with the polish of his craft. The distinction between old and new songs is somewhat blurred: in those days, 'culture' did not have to be old, and as Burns' fame grew, his songs became culture before the ink was dry.

It is significant that while he hoped to make money from his poems, he never took payment for his songs. Throughout the six volumes of the *Scots Musical Museum* – published collections of Scottish songs – he edited from 1787 and to which he was the principal contributor, he took only £10: an initial £5, and a further £5 when, on his deathbed, he wrote a letter to his collaborator George Thomson begging for help with a tailor's bill.

Despite its dusty title, the *Musical Museum* did not mean a storehouse of the old. 'Museum' literally meant the home of the Muses, the nine patrons of the arts from Greek mythology.

In the autumn of 1784 Rob was called to the kirk to face public condemnation for Lizzie Paton's condition. On this occasion, he was not required to sit upon the 'creepie stool' – the three-legged stool retained for the public display of sinners. At the end of the sermon, however, he had to stand up and be harangued by the Minister for the sin of 'houghmagandie' – fornication. The sinner would sometimes answer back: it is recorded that Rob remained silent.

At about this time, Rob met one Jean Armour, a Mauchline lass of good family, whose father was a master-mason. The story of their first meeting is charming – and has no basis in fact. During Race Week in April 1784, Rob had gone to a local dance. As ever, his faithful dog – there always was one – trotted at his heels. The dog, however, got in the way of the dancers and

Rob sent him off home with the remark: 'I wish I could find a lass that would love me as well as my dog' – a line, of course, quite calculated to excite any lass that cared to pick up the challenge. Jean Armour did. A few days later, walking through Mauchline, Rob heard the saucy remark: 'Well, Mossgiel, have you gotten any lass yet to love you as well as your dog?'

Jean was not then – indeed ever – the only romantic interest in Rob's life and the Armours were frankly appalled at the blithe and forward way in which their daughter seemed to pursue this worthless young man – not only was he an unsuccessful farmer and the father of a bastard, a man who had already faced public

Jean Armour and granddaughter Sarah

humiliation in the kirk but worse, he was beginning to be known locally as Rob the Rhymer. Parental indignation was unconfined.

The farm at Mossgiel had been a bitter disappointment. In the first year, the unlucky purchase of bad seed was to blame; in the second year, a late harvest.

At about this time, Rob became fascinated with the prospect of emigration to Jamaica. The reasons may have been many – Mossgiel was not the runaway success he'd hoped, he chafed against the petty restrictions of kirk morality, the complications of his personal life seemed a burden and would become more so – though it is equally likely that at first Jamaica simply appealed for all the reasons people always seek escape: freedom, adventure, money.

But the Jamaica trip had to be financed somehow, and so grew the idea of publishing, on subscription, a volume of his poems.

Early in 1786, Jean Armour had become pregnant: Mr Armour, it is recorded, swooned away at the worst news he could imagine. Pregnancy outside wedlock was as common in eighteenth-century Scotland as elsewhere: indeed, in farming communities it made practical sense to ensure a bride's fertility before committing to marriage. Scots law conveniently bestowed retroactive legitimacy on children born before their parents' marriage.

Jean Armour was not unusual in her unmarried pregnant state: but her parents had decent hopes for her, and a bankrupt poet was not among them. Moreover, Jean produced a document for their approval: a paper willingly signed by Rob which under Scots law constituted a marriage document. One can imagine the state of Mr Armour's blood pressure as Jean was packed off to relatives in Paisley.

Parental anger and her own vulnerable condition probably combined to make the beleaguered Jean 'confess' to Mauchline Kirk and 'repent' her sins. She handed the marriage document over to her parents who defaced it so as to remove its legal status.

Rob interpreted her behaviour as rejection and desertion, and turned against her with something very like venom. This stage of their relationship is marked by vivid dramas of renunciation and grand gestures. Burns adopted an attitude – and then came to believe in it absolutely.

Typically, he regarded the whole sorry business as entirely Jean's fault and sought to justify his own actions. When she did return to Mauchline, he wrote to a friend:

'Poor, ill-advised, ungrateful Armour came home on Friday last ... what she thinks of her conduct I don't know; one thing I know, she has made me completely miserable. Never man loved a woman more than I did her; and, to confess a truth ... I still do love her. It is not the losing her that makes me unhappy, but for her sake I feel most severely ... May God forgive her ingratitude and perjury to me. Sanctimoniously he recorded that I foresee that she is on the road to eternal ruin.'

Burns appears to have been so absorbed by his own emotions and feelings, to the exclusion of other people's sense of reality, that he would react with surprise when anyone else displayed a positive reaction to anything he said or did. That summer of 1786 Burns thundered: 'Against two things I am as fixed as fate; staying at home [that is, Mossgiel] and owning her conjugally. The first, by Heaven, I will not do! The last, by Hell, I will never do!' Eventually, of course, he did both.

In that same summer of 1786, however, Rob was telling a friend that yet another woman – quite possibly 'Highland Mary' – was pregnant by him, while Jean, it seemed, was carrying twins. Her father was implacable in his hatred of Rob. The farm was definitely a failure. Suddenly, a Jamaica-bound ship must have seemed overwhelmingly attractive.

The enigmatic figure of Highland Mary glows from a dark corner of Burns' life and has remained a powerful part of the legend. The known facts are few. Margaret Campbell originally came from Dunoon, in Argyll, and had arrived in Mauchline to work as a nursemaid in the home of Burns' friend and benefactor, Gavin Hamilton. She is described as tall and fair-haired, with blue eyes and a pleasant and winning manner.

Burns had been writing to a friend – concerning Jean's 'desertion' – that he was 'wiping away the grief-worn eye ... to look for another wife'. Burns' own recollection of their affair is not to be relied on in detail but probably in emotion:

'My Highland lassie was a warm-hearted, charming young creature
as ever blessed a man with generous love'.

His song, *The Highland Lassie O*, was written for her.

In May 1786 Mary went to stay with relatives in Greenock, and Burns gave her a two-volume Bible as a parting gift. The inscription inside, in Rob's bold hand, urged fidelity, and this exchange of Bibles has been interpreted by some as a sort of marriage contract. He seems to have planned to take Mary with him to Jamaica, where they would start a new life together: why then did Mary leave Mauchline and return to Greenock? Officially, it was to prepare for her trip. In October, however, Burns received an anonymous letter from Greenock telling him that Mary was dead.

Mystery surrounds the cause of her death. Her family thereafter displayed implacable hostility to Burns and it is likely they destroyed his letters to Mary, but with good business sense, they held on to the Bibles which were ultimately sold for a satisfactory sum of money.

Mary was buried in Greenock, and in 1803 the Greenock Burns Club noted a resolution to erect a stone in her memory. In 1920, however, the graveyard was cleared for building and Mary Campbell's grave opened.

Among the remains was found part of a child's coffin, and this has fuelled the belief that what caused Mary's death was not in fact a fever, but childbirth, and that the child died with her. This would, of course, explain to some extent the hostility felt by her family towards Robert Burns.

When he was not being openly boastful about his sexual conquests, Burns could be extraordinarily secretive: and he took the latter path with Mary Campbell. Her death seems to have plunged him into a violent spasm of grief, and in later years his frequent bouts of depression would be accompanied by anguish when 'with speechless agony of rapture again [I] recognise my lost, my ever dear Mary!' A poem by Burns, *Thou lingering Star*, has been re-titled *To Mary in Heaven* by Burns scholars, an oddly pious title which suggests that Mary remained for ever a constant inspiration to Burns. A cynic might add: well, of course she would, she was dead.

Burns might dedicate his poems to women, but these women's names were often but convenient hooks upon which to hang an existing idea for a poem or a song. No artist is ever really inspired by anything but his or her own talent. Burns was not the first, and would not be the last, artist to look back wistfully to a 'perfect' relationship with an 'ideal' lover long and conveniently dead and thus immobile for ever in that perfection, and find the accompanying emotions of loss, regret, pain and longing a fertile stimulus for art.

But another child of Burns was in the womb that summer, certainly the one he cared about most: the first volume of his poems. Such a child was the only one that could command his absolute loyalty, and his continued presence in Scotland.

On 31 July 1786 John Wilson of Kilmarnock printed 600 copies of a book called *Scottish Poems* by Robert Burns. It cost three shillings and bore a dedication to his landlord, Gavin Hamilton. Burns' reputation had been growing steadily in Ayrshire but the success of this first volume must have surprised everyone: it was an overnight success. It has been estimated that Burns probably made about £50 from this first collection – his second volume, published in Edinburgh the following year, earned him about £800.

This sudden success seems to have encouraged Mr Armour to view Rob in a different light as a prospective son-in-law. But Rob was cool with Jean, who gave birth to twins, a boy and a girl, in September.

So Highland Mary sank back into the shadows of the past, and on 27 November 1786, Rob set out for Edinburgh – where his reputation as a poet had already preceded him. He was seeking a change in his fortune: and if all else failed, a ship for the West Indies sailed from Leith just before Christmas.

4 – *Edinburgh: Burns in Love 1786-8*

'For my own part I never had the least thought or inclination of turning Poet until I got heartily in Love, and then Rhyme & Song were, in a manner, the spontaneous language of my heart.'

But Edinburgh was not a failure. An image had been stored in the popular imagination, and Edinburgh society fell in love with it – the 'Heav'n-taught' ploughman whose deceptively unsophisticated lyrics had a wide popular appeal, to servant and master – and mistress – alike.

The Edinburgh society to which Burns had access – not least because of his Freemasonry – was self-consciously elegant, fashionable and intellectual. Great men cast their shadow everywhere: David Hume, the philosopher and author of *A Treatise of Human Nature*, was but 10 years in his grave: Adam Smith had only just moved to London in search of a cure for his chronic bowel obstruction, undoubtedly the consequence of a life devoted to the study of political economy. Henry Dundas, Lord President of the Court of Session and the 'uncrowned King of Scotland', ruled Scotland in the name of the Prime Minister, William Pitt.

Burns bore Dundas a personal grudge: advised by a friend that it would make good sense to write a poem in praise of the great man, Rob did so. His innate pride and dignity did not make Rob a natural sycophant, and he seems to have accepted the need to lubricate his career path with such flatteries sourly.

In this instance, however, it backfired. Dundas completely ignored Rob's poem and its covering letter and never bothered to reply. Hurt pride ensured that Burns never forgot the slight.

Of personal importance to Burns were his friendships with his hero, the novelist Henry Mackenzie – who largely orchestrated the Ploughman Poet myth – and the publisher William Creech. On 21 April 1787 Creech published what is known as the First Edinburgh Edition of Burns' poems. Over-subscribed on publication, Creech had to reprint almost immediately. In all, 3000 copies were printed.

What was he like, this Ayrshire farmer without whom no gathering of the rich and famous was complete? Expecting a rough ploughman, whom did they really meet? Portraits of Burns suggest an open, candid face, too perpetually boyish to be handsome. He was of medium height and years at the plough had given him a slight stoop; exposure to the weather in all seasons made his complexion darker and coarser than was fashionable – the rich had pale, delicate skins upon which the wind never blew. Contemporary accounts describe Burns as being particular in his dress, whatever his financial circumstances; neat without being dandyish, he tied his black hair in a ponytail and never adopted the Edinburgh habit of using powder on it.

Two of Burns' features were so striking that many who met him felt moved to comment on them. His eyes were large, dark and, according to the 15-year-old Walter Scott, glowing with life. 'I never saw such another eye in a human head', he wrote in boyish awe. Josiah Walker, an early biographer, wrote that 'It [his eye] was full of mind'. And his speaking voice was, apparently, equally attractive: 'melodic and expressive'. In her memoir of Burns, Maria Riddell wrote: 'The rapid lightnings of his eye were always the harbingers of some flash of genius ... his voice alone could improve upon the magic of his eye ... it alternately captivated the ear with the melody of poetic numbers, the perspicuity of nervous reasoning, or the ardent sallies of enthusiastic patriotism.'

Although he was always somewhat accident-prone, he seems to have been a self-possessed and warmly attractive man who refused to play the part of the grateful recipient of Edinburgh's graciousness. This did not please everyone. At a time when polite manners tended to be artificial as well as superficial, Burns' steady gaze was unnerving. Even his sponsor, Henry Mackenzie described him as 'a little too independent of his mind for his station'.

The women, too, were of a different sort – not servant girls and farmers' daughters, and a million miles from Jean Armour. Women like Jane Duchess of Gordon, educated, witty and as free as only money and class could make them, impressed him mightily.

One woman of importance to Burns during this Edinburgh period – probably of great importance – was Peggy Chalmers, a farmer's daughter and a distant relative of Burns' friend Gavin Hamilton. They may have met early in 1787, when Burns was a newly published poet. They did meet again in Edinburgh, however, and Burns wrote the song *My Peggy's Charms* for her. In October that year, touring the Highlands, Burns spent eight days with Peggy at Harviestoun. He proposed marriage to her: she rejected him, but they remained on affectionate terms, and continued to write to each other until her marriage to an Edinburgh banker in 1788.

Burns' feelings for her are expressed in one of these letters: '... When I think I have met with you, and have lived more of real life with you in eight days than I can do with almost anybody I meet with in eight years – when I think of the improbability of meeting you in this world again – I could sit down and cry like a child!'

With her ability to be both an intellectual companion as well as a physical one, Peggy's refusal of his proposal may seem curious. This may in part have been because of her existing 'understanding' with Lewis Hay, whom she subsequently married: class may also have been an issue. Rob was a farmer whose wife needed to work in the dairy and the garden, and this practical role would have been out of the question for the cultivated Miss Chalmers.

Within weeks of his arrival in the capital, Burns had commenced a passionate friendship with one Agnes McLehose, a surgeon's daughter and the niece of Lord Craig. The affair was largely conducted by letter and in correspondence the lovestruck couple became 'Clarinda' and 'Sylvander'. In 1776 the 17-year-old Clarinda had married one James McLehose, a law agent, and by 1780 was the mother of four babies. It was an unhappy marriage, however,

Clarinda's Grave – Canongate Cemetery

and McLehose eventually deserted his wife for a black mistress and a plantation in Jamaica.

Agnes took a house in Potter Row, near the medical school in Edinburgh, and there established herself, with her uncle – a judge – as her social guardian and protector. Clarinda wrote poetry herself and was educated enough to take a critical view of Burns' own poetry. She was immediately smitten by him at their first meeting in December 1787, and invited him to tea.

Burns was prevented from coming by an injury to his knee – a drunken coachman caused him to fall from a coach. Frustrated at not seeing each other, they began a rapid and eloquent exchange of letters. Their love was consummated in correspondence and not in fact: Agnes was, after all, married and a member of Edinburgh society mindful of her status and the expectations of her position. It was not only Clarinda's married status that prevented a more conventional relationship, but social class as well – as was the problem with all the other educated, intelligent women Burns encountered in Edinburgh society. Intellectually he might be their superior, but socially he would always be their inferior – no more perhaps than a bit of celebrity rough. And he would never be allowed to forget that fact.

Initially at least, this lack of a physical dimension probably did nothing more than add a charge of excitement to the friendship between Burns and Clarinda. As the months passed, their letters became more and more passionate: 'You are an angel, Clarinda ... to kiss your hand, to live on your smile ... I propose to keep sacred set times to wander in the woods and wilds for meditation on you.'

Emotionally wrapped up in a dream of love, Burns was not however the man to enjoy platonic relationships for long – and Clarinda sensed this. 'I esteem you', he wrote to Clarinda, 'I love you as a friend ... I love you as a woman beyond any one in all the circle of creation'. This letter goes on in a similar vein of rapture for some time. Years later, against a copy of this letter, Burns was to write: 'Fustian rant!'

He began to inhabit two Edinburghs: the drawing-rooms of the rich and famous, and the salty taverns of the Royal Mile and the Grassmarket, where he could be himself. The relationship between Sylvander and his Clarinda might be a communion of minds, but Rob Burns' affairs with May Cameron and Jenny Clow, both servant girls, were emphatically not. Both women became pregnant, and both issued writs against Burns to ensure he acknowledged paternity.

His injured knee recovered, Burns took to the saddle for the first of the tours to other parts of Scotland that he made during this Edinburgh period. With his friend Robert Ainslie he visited the Border counties: East Lothian, Berwick, Roxburgh, Selkirk and Dumfries. They travelled east to west, and of course called in at Mossgiel and Mauchline, where Burns sought out Jean Armour. Jean's honestly physical response to him must have seemed a refreshing change from the mannered eyelash-fluttering of Edinburgh.

Returning to the capital, Burns set out almost immediately for the north, starting from Linlithgow and Stirling. His companion this time was his friend *Kind honest-hearted Willie* – William Nicol, master of classics at Edinburgh's High School – though they had some fierce disagreements on their trip.

Throughout his life, Burns had the delightful habit of scratching spontaneous thoughts on window-panes with his diamond ring. Passing through Stirling and in an excess of fervour for the lost glamour of the Stewart kings, now replaced by a beef-witted German dynasty from Hanover, he wrote:

Stewarts once in glory reign'd'
And laws for Scotland's weal ordained ...
A race outlandish fills their throne:
An idiot race, to honour lost –
Who know them best despise them most.

At this time, Burns was exploiting what influence he could to obtain what was virtually a civil service job, as an Exciseman – a collector of local taxation. Remembering by whom a civil servant is ultimately employed, Burns returned to Stirling a fortnight later and smashed the offending window.

Blair Castle – Burns stayed here in 1788 (see next page)

The travellers' destination was Kincardine, where the Burns' family roots were, but in travelling back to the land of his forbearers, Burns was entertained in some style, staying at Blair Castle with the Duke and Duchess of Atholl, and Gordon Castle with the enigmatic Duchess Jane.

In 1788 Burns' Edinburgh period came to an end. He had been feted and lionised, and hailed by the Freemasons as 'Caledonia's Bard'. He had made some money from his poems, but he needed a job – the growing brood of children for whom he took responsibility needed a more reliable source of income than poetry. Nor was he comfortable with the role of tame rustic which had been created for him: his pride rebelled against it. 'How wretched is the man that hangs on and by the favours of the great!' he wrote – and believed.

Early in that year he headed west again to deal with two urgent matters at home: the possibility of a new farm at Ellisland, and Jean Armour, heavily pregnant with the second set of twins which had been the legacy of their reunion the previous year.

Jean's family had thrown her out: Mr Armour had undergone a change of heart and Burns' fame, celebrity and – he thought – money now made him seem a more suitable son-in-law. During that brief return to Ayrshire in 1787 he had hoped to trap Burns into a formal marriage with Jean. The fact that she immediately gave herself to him and became pregnant again was the last straw. Feeling that her passionate response showed a lamentable lack of calculation and strategy, the Armours told her to leave their home. She was in a sad and desperate plight, and only Rob could save her – quite literally.

In Edinburgh, though, he had Clarinda. In December 1787 he had written to a friend: 'Almighty Love still reigns and revels in my bosom; and I am at this moment ready to hang myself for a young Edinburgh widow' – widow not being quite accurate.

In February, returning to Mossgiel to make arrangements for Jean's confinement, he wrote to Bob Ainslie: 'I found Jean ... destitute and friendless; all for the good old cause: I have reconciled her to her fate: I have reconciled her to her mother: I have taken her a room: I have taken her to my arms: I have given her a mahogany bed; I have given her a guinea; and I have f——d her till she rejoiced with joy unspeakable and full of glory ... But ... I swore her ... solemnly never to attempt any claim on me as a husband ... She did all this, like a good girl, and I took the opportunity of some dry horse-litter, and gave her such a thundering scalade that electrified the very marrow of her bones.' Poor Jean! Somehow, yet again, Burns made it all seem entirely her fault, and bestowing on her the supreme gift of his body was supposed to make it all right.

On 3 March, Jean gave birth to twins: they both died.

Burns left for Edinburgh, and for Clarinda, again. But in March he was back in Mauchline, seeing to farm business and pursuing his hopes of an Excise career.

He wrote to Clarinda: 'I ... called for a certain woman. I am disgusted with her! I cannot endure her! I .... tried to compare her with my Clarinda ...' Burns concluded that it was like comparing a penny candle with the 'cloudless glory of the meridian sun'. He went on to rail against Jean's 'vulgarity of soul' and 'tasteless insipidity', saying that 'I have done with her and she with me'.

Six weeks later, he had married Jean. He did not tell Clarinda, but left her to find out from his friend Robert Ainslie.

In a letter he crowed: 'I am so enamoured with a certain girl's twin-bearing merit that I have given her a legal right to the best blood in my body.' As for Clarinda, busy at her desk in Edinburgh pouring out letter after letter of undying love and affection, the news of his marriage came second-hand. Burns himself did not write to her for a year. That body blow may be imagined – from the distance of 200 years, it has lost none of its hurt. The letter he wrote to her that year later is described as an essay in self-justification and contains nothing which suggests even a faint awareness of the pain he had caused her.

It has been suggested that Burns' need for employment, and the offer from the Excise, lay behind his sudden change of heart over Jean: he was obliged to regularise his position. Marrying Jean may also have been a recognition of his need for honest physical affection set beside Clarinda's arm's-length letter writing. Whatever the truth may be, it is a cruel incident in the life of a man generally kind – but contradiction was ever the key to Burns' character.

By 1790, Clarinda and Sylvander had resumed their correspondence and Burns was again writing to her as 'my ever-beloved, my ever-sacred'. On

6 December 1791, five years before Burns' death, they met in Edinburgh for the last time. This meeting led to the writing of *Ae Fond Kiss*, one of Burns' finest lyrics.

'Love,' Burns wrote, 'is the Alpha and Omega of human enjoyment.' Agnes McLehose seems to have understood him very well. She once told him, with great insight: 'You are so formed you cannot be happy without a tender attachment'. Her use of the singular is the only incorrect note there. Having read Burns' 'autobiography' – a letter written to Dr John Moore, and now in the British Museum – she commented that she could find 'not a trace of friendship towards a female,' adding that the long-suffering Jean Armour must be 'either an angel or a dolt'.

Burns' passion for Clarinda cooled, but she seems to have retained a place in her heart for him for ever, and became increasingly devout in old age. In 1831, some 40 years after Burns' death, she wrote on the anniversary of their last meeting: '...this day I never can forget. Parted with Burns never more to meet in this world. Oh, may we meet in heaven.'

5 – Ellisland 1788-91

'– and so, farewell to rakery'

Rob's adult life entered a third phase. Six miles north of the market town of Dumfries lies Ellisland. In 1788 there wasn't even a farmhouse there. Rob built the existing house himself, with £300 supplied by his landlord Patrick Miller of Dalswinton, living meanwhile in a damp hut on the land.

The young married man was alone, too, for Jean remained behind in Ayrshire with her son Robert – this small Rob being the only survivor of the first set of twins, the little girl Jean having died. He missed his wife and child, and when time allowed he would make the journey to see them in Mauchline on horseback – Jean would walk part of the way to meet him, and ride behind him when they met up.

The foundation stone of Ellisland was laid according to proper masonic rites. It was built as a family home and a working farmhouse where hams would be smoked and cheese made, but there was also a room with a desk

Ellisland

and a chair where he could write – and the Ellisland years were remarkably productive. Over 130 poems and songs, including *Tam O' Shanter*, were written here as well as some 230 letters to his widening circle of correspondents.

In addition to building a home for his family, the land required intensive labour. When Rob took up the tenancy it still had the 'corrugated' appearance of the old runrig system of agriculture, the land being divided into narrow strips raised in the middle to allow drainage. He applied himself to the widening of these rigs so they would drain more efficiently and the quality of the soil could be improved with lime. But the soil was poor as well as stony, and Burns saw what financial resources he had seep away into it – he was already short of money, having saved his brother Gilbert from bankruptcy.

Finally, the Excise post came through, and Rob embarked upon an entirely new career as a 'gauger' or measurer, an officer of His Majesty's Excise. His name was entered on the Excise list with the annotation: 'Never tryed; a Poet'. In order to have time for this, he changed Ellisland from an arable to a dairy farm, so that Jean could supervise the milking and the cheese-making. Burns is generally credited with the introduction of the Ayrshire dairy cow to the Dumfries area.

In the days before income tax, Excise was a tax levied on home-produced goods, similar to today's VAT. It was levied on essentials, such as salt, soap, candles and paper, as well as on luxuries such as whisky and tobacco – on both accounts, a most unpopular tax.

The Exciseman travelled his patch, checking on the makers and merchants of these taxable goods and literally measuring the amount of tax to be paid. An element of surprise was often necessary in these visits.

His territory covered ten parishes in Dumfriesshire and he often rode 200 miles a week, attending all the county fairs and gatherings. Good relations with the local magistrates, through Freemasonry, undoubtedly helped him in the discharge of his duties. At the end of a probationary period that same supervisor who wondered how a poet would cope with the job wrote: 'Turns out well'.

The disadvantage of this demanding work was, however, the tax it levied on Burns' own health and time. Although this proved to be one of the most fertile and creative periods of his writing life – *Tam o' Shanter* is said to have been written in a single day – a hard day in the saddle, in all weathers, with reports to write in the evening, left him with little energy. Physically he was already in terminal decline, and he stumbled into sloughs of black depression and anxiety, obsessed with a fear of poverty and thoughts of death.

Despite Burns' rage at Jean and his rejection of her before their marriage, he had been unable to abandon her entirely, and their married life was considerably happier than their courtship. Jean, for her part, seems content to have been Mrs Burns, and took over the practical management of Ellisland during the long hours Rob was away.

It is known that Jean had a fine singing voice – the 'finest wood-note wild' – a quality Burns always found attractive in women, and 14 of Burns' poems are supposed to be about her. A letter in 1788 provides an interesting insight into the foundation of their relationship which rings true: the marriage was, wrote Burns, 'not in consequence of the attachment of romance perhaps; but I had a long and much-loved fellow creature's happiness or misery in my determination, and I durst not trifle with so important a deposit. Nor have I any cause to repent it ... I have got the handsomest figure, the sweetest temper ... and kindest heart in the county.' In song he wrote:

It may escape the courtly sparks
It may escape the learned clerks;
But weel the watching lover marks
The kind love that's in her e'e.

And, of course, to Burns' satisfaction: 'Mrs Burns believes, as firmly as her creed, that I am *le plus bel esprit*...'

We should remember too that Burns lived long before the Victorian era banished sex to a silent underworld: this was a more candid age. He wrote both poetry and prose expressing his enjoyment of physical love, which he called 'the Tree of Life between Man and Woman' – though his language was not always so high-minded. 'Oh, what a peacemaker is a guid weel-willy pintle!' he wrote at a turbulent time in his relationship with Jean Armour. One of many delightfully bawdy songs is *Come Rede me Dame*:

Come rede me, dame, come tell me, dame
My dame come tell me truly
What length o' graith, when weel ca'd hame,
Will sair a woman duly?
The carlin clew her wanton tail
Her wanton tail sae ready -
I learn'd a song in Annandale,
Nine inch will please a lady.

A pet project while at Ellisland was the founding, with his friend and neighbour Robert Riddell, of the first circulating library known to the area.

It was open to all upon payment of a five-shilling membership fee – sixpence thereafter at monthly meetings – and the proceeds went towards the purchase of books which could be borrowed on a first-come, first-served basis. Burns managed this venture with conspicuous commitment.

Visitors to Ellisland remarked upon Burns' apparent ease in his domestic circle and his farming role. His affection towards Jean was noted, as were the pet sheep, the extravagance of feeding potatoes to the cows and the fact that the servants ate every bit as well as the family – and that was well. Jean wore kid gloves to church and Burns was as contradictory as ever when, calling himself a farmer and an Exciseman, he nonetheless inscribed 'Robert Burns Poet' on the collar of his dog.

But the spongy ground of Ellisland never repaid the care and the outlay lavished upon it, and Rob did not have the capital to keep pouring into its boggy soil. He was never a bad farmer, but he was a singularly unlucky one.

There were, as ever, money worries. Whatever he could earn or save had been soaked up by his farming disasters and by his responsibilities. His family grew with the birth of Francis in 1789 and William in 1791, while Anna Park, barmaid at the Globe Inn in Dumfries, would add another infant to his brood of babies born outside his marriage. Jean Armour took Anna Park's child into her own home to care for with the apparently nonchalant remark that 'Our Robbie should have had twa wives.'

Globe Inn, Dumfries

In February 1791, he fell with his horse and broke his arm. In the summer, clumsy as ever, he injured his leg in another accident. In November, he finally gave up on Ellisland – 'a ruinous business' – and the farmer's life and moved into Dumfries.

The loss of Ellisland was a bitter blow for Rob – and unusually strained relations with Jean for a while, who blamed him for it. He moved his family to a house that is now 11 Bank Street, Dumfries, their possessions loaded on carts, with Jean's pet heifer trotting behind.

One anecdote indicates more than anything the bitterness he felt. At Ellisland he had freely indulged his passion for scribbling verse on the window panes. Remembering this upon arrival in Dumfries, he despatched his brother-in-law to return and smash every window so inscribed. He would not leave his verse behind in a place that had so broken his heart.

6 – The Gauger 1791-6

My poetry will outlast my poverty

As with every enterprise in his life, Burns gave himself to his work with the Excise with vigour and diligence. Although one can find quotations in which he describes this task as 'execrable office of whipper-in to the bloodhounds of justice' it's as well to remember that Burns was something of a chameleon in his mood swings, capable of expressing extremes of opinion in different letters to different people on the same day. Influential friends may have won him the Excise job, but his own competence kept it.

The evidence is that he was as careful and workmanlike in stamping leather and measuring malt vats as he was in writing poems. The Excise tax was hated and times were hard: smuggling and illicit stills were but two ways to circumvent it. The job of an Exciseman carried risk and sometimes violence. Like his brother officers, Burns was armed: his brace of pistols may be seen today in his Birthplace Museum. Shortly before his death, Burns gave them to his Dumfries doctor, William Maxwell. This Dr Maxwell was not only his doctor but his friend, and had led a colourful life. A native Scot educated in France, where he studied medicine, he had been one of the National Guard present at the execution of Louis XVI.

In 1792, Burns was promoted to the First or Port Division of the Dumfries Excise. His patch could now be covered on foot, and his pay was £70 a year with the possibility of up to £20 extra in bonuses.

The *Edinburgh Evening Courant* of 8 March that year carried news of an exciting raid in the Solway Firth, which had taken place a week earlier. A smuggling brig *Rosamond* was stranded by the tide in the Firth, and Burns, at the head of a party of armed dragoons, attempted to board her. It being too dangerous to commit horses to the treacherous sands, he led his men chest-deep into the freezing waters. They were continuously under fire from the smugglers, until – with the Excise 100 yards from the vessel – they gave up and legged it over the side and for England.

The contents of the *Rosamond* went to public auction, and Burns bought four carronades – small cannon – which he then donated to the French Legislative Assembly. It was a cavalier gesture of solidarity with a revolutionary cause – quite apart from the fact that they cost a great deal of money which he could not afford.

These were the closing years of his life: both physically and mentally, he was often in great distress. But Burns was a man of mercurial spirits. Whatever his private anguish – and his capacity for it was considerable – he was a man engaged with life and the business of life. Playing with his children or talking with company in the pubs of Dumfries – the Globe Inn or the King's Head – he soon regained that graceful warmth which drew people to him.

Part of this commitment to life was Burns' passion for politics. All his life he would champion egalitarianism and justice in society, and thus any cause he saw as representing these principles. It was this passion that enabled him to embrace quite opposing principles without thinking things through: he could be both a Jacobite and anti-royalist, as he was in his support of the French Revolution. In later generations, workers' movements would claim Burns for their own. Keir Hardie, founder of the British Labour movement, wrote that he 'owed more to Burns than to any man, living or dead'.

Revolution was the backdrop to Burns' life. He was 17 when the American War of Independence started in 1776, and an ardent supporter of the American cause. As a Jacobite, he had no loyalty to the German dynasty in London. Moreover, two of the heroes of that revolution – Benjamin Franklin and George Washington – were Freemasons. Once again, it seemed that Freemasonry was the natural intellectual home of all right-thinking men who championed equality and freedom.

During his career as an Exciseman, and therefore a hired hand of the government, Burns was often in hot water because of his radical political views. On more than one occasion he was forced to retract or apologise for something said or written when faced with the threat of losing that desperately needed income. There is a theory that some of the more radical poems he wrote in these Dumfries years were destroyed at his death by well-meaning friends, anxious not to jeopardize Jean's future financial security as the widow of an Exciseman.

One example of this recklessness on the part of a civil servant came at a large gathering of establishment figures when a toast was proposed to the Prime Minister Pitt. Burns suggested they raise their glasses instead to 'the health of a better man, George Washington'.

In October 1792, after a performance of *As You Like It* at the Theatre Royal in Dumfries, a group of radicals began to sing the French revolutionary song *Ça Ira* – and Burns joined in. Denounced as disloyal, another apology followed, and more bile was swallowed only in the interests of his family's income.

In Dumfries, Burns became involved in local politics to the extent of writing ballads supporting the local Tory candidate against the Whig candidate sponsored by the Duke of Queensberry – although he later changed and became a Whig supporter. In the Duke, Burns saw the archetype of the wicked aristocrat: self-indulgent and opulent in lifestyle, and a bad landlord. Aristocrats such as the Duke were having a bad time in France, and Burns watched events in that country with delight.

In 1789 the Bastille was stormed and in 1793 Louis XVI and Marie Antoinette went to the guillotine. Burns wrote of the latter event: 'What is there in the delivering over of a perjured Blockhead and an unprincipled prostitute into the hands of the hangman ...' It is an uncharacteristically bloodthirsty comment for a man who was so resolutely anti-war and hated violence.

'War,' he once said, 'I deprecate: misery and ruin to thousands are in the blast that announces the destructive demon.' And, with a typically light reference to a favoured pastime, 'I am better pleased to make one more than be the death of 20.'

In 1791, Burns met another educated, socially superior woman with whom he conducted a platonic though ardent friendship. Maria Riddell was English, born in 1772 and thus 13 years Burns' junior, and the daughter of the Governor of the Leeward Islands. In 1790 she had married Walter Riddell who owned sugar plantations in the West Indies, and in 1792 they moved to Scotland with their two daughters, buying an estate they renamed Woodley Park – Woodley was Maria's maiden name – near Dumfries.

Like other cultured ladies of taste and education, Maria wrote poetry and imagined herself artistic – she had after all published a book about the Leeward Islands. Her brother-in-law Robert Riddell owned Friar's Carse, an estate north of the Burns farm at Ellisland, and Burns was a frequent visitor. The two men had music as a common bond. Here, in 1791, Maria and Robert met; by April 1793 she was 'thou first of Friends'. Sending her the poem *The last time I came o'er the moor* Burns comments revealingly: 'It is but a cold, inanimate composition. It will be absolutely necessary for me to get in love, else I shall never be able to make a line worth reading on the subject.'

They met frequently until an incident at Friar's Carse led to an estrangement. Various accounts are given of this incident, at which Maria was not present, but it involved a drunken Burns and 'inappropriate' behaviour towards Robert Riddell's frosty English wife. Although this incident is sometimes called 'The Rape of the Sabine Women' it sounds no more than the boisterous rowdiness that may accompany a robust consumption of drink – but Burns' English hosts were not amused at all by this affront to upper-class manners. For a while Burns was not invited to Friar's Carse and Maria felt obliged by family loyalty to cold-shoulder him. This caused Burns a great deal of torment: 'In a face where I used to meet the kind complacency of friendly confidence, now to find cold neglect and contemptuous scorn – is a wrench that my heart can ill bear.'

By 1795 they were, however, reconciled. Maria was now living with her husband at Tinwald House, between Dumfries and Lochmaben – Woodley Park had been lost by his financial improvidence.

After Burns' death, Maria proved a true friend to his memory. She wrote a generous memoir for the *Dumfries Weekly Journal* which was reprinted widely and alludes to his personal failings with the sensible comment: 'the world must have continued very stationary in its intellectual acquirements, had it never given birth to any but men of plain sense.' Maria died in 1808, 12 years after Burns, at the age of 36.

Burns established himself as a popular figure in Dumfries. His social circle was always wide and his Dumfries friends included a farrier as well as the Collector of Stamp Duties. From boyhood he was always willing to put his

Burns House, Dumfries

literary skills at the service of others, and here too he continued to compose letters for those who asked: letters of love, of pursuit or of business.

With the birth of a son James in 1794, he and Jean now had a family of four boys – Elizabeth, the only surviving daughter who was Rob's particular treasure, had been born in 1793 and the family moved to a larger, geranium-brick house in Mill Vennel, now called Burns Street. There were two rooms upstairs, and the room he shared with Jean had a box-bed similar to the one he'd been born in, with a cradle on the floor beside it, scarcely ever empty. Off this room was a tiny study for writing, in which he scratched his name on the window.

The big family Bible – now in the Birthplace Museum – contains details of the births of all their children written in Rob's big distinctive hand – all except the birth of Maxwell, the son born on the day of his funeral and named in honour of his doctor.

Family life absorbed him. He enjoyed the time spent directing the education of his boys. As for Jean, he was anxious that his wife should be well-dressed – she who was so occupied with children and a household. She was one of the first women in Dumfries to follow that elegant new trend and wear a gingham dress.

The start of the war with France in 1793 affected the Excise business and his income dropped. Burns' health suffered accordingly. He described his affliction by the 'terrible trinity – Rheumatism, Cold and Fever'.

His political sympathies again caused him distress in this year of 1793. In August Thomas Muir of Huntershill, Glasgow, a lawyer of liberal sympathies, was brought to trial. His crime was sedition: the jury found him guilty as charged, of distributing copies of Thomas Paine's *The Rights of Man*, a banned book. Among other things, Paine inveighed against the tradition of inherited wealth and status in France and in Britain. Burns himself owned a copy and had read it with profound admiration. Muir was sentenced to 14 years' transportation, a severe sentence that was meant to shock and to warn.

There is evidence that Burns felt duly shocked and warned – deeply depressed by the values of the society in which he lived, but to whom he owed his meat and drink. Burns and his friend John Syme were in Gatehouse of Fleet when Muir was led through in chains, on his way to a show trial in Edinburgh.

A direct result of Thomas Muir's sentence was the song *Scots wha' hae wi' Wallace bled*. From boyhood, Burns had had a fascination for William Wallace, the thirteenth-century hero of Scottish independence. He later wrote: 'The story of Wallace poured a Scottish prejudice in my veins which will boil along there till the flood-gates of life shut in eternal rest.' Forbidden in 1793 from paying open tribute to Muir, Burns looked back to another man who had paid dearly for standing up before tyranny.

His bitterness at being unable to express his personal views as publicly as he would wish led to the composition of these telling lines:

> In Politics if thou would'st mix
> And mean thy fortunes be;
> Bear this in mind, be deaf and blind,
> Let great folks hear and see.

The literary task which continued to occupy most of Rob's time was his collaboration with James Johnson, a music publisher, and George Thomson, an Edinburgh civil servant and gifted musician, on the *Scots Musical Museum*. His friend Robert Riddell was a more than competent musician, and Rob learned immensely from him, eventually outstripping both his collaborators with his musical polish and style. In a letter of 1793 Burns described the essence of a ballad as being simplicity, but he himself took great pains with even the simplest of lyrics, knowing how hard true simplicity is to achieve. *Auld Lang Syne* was first published in one of these volumes.

The war with France dragged on, and in 1795 Burns joined the Royal Dumfries Volunteers, a democratically run militia. There was a splendid uniform with a red braided jacket and white breeches, but the tailor's bill for £7 4s threw Burns into a frenzy of despair. As always, he vented his fury in verse:

> What ails ye now, ye lousie bitch,
> To thresh my back at sic a pitch?

The final years are clouded by money worries. Stepping into another man's shoes as a district supervisor carried with it the burden of additional work and responsibility, which he discharged with competence and efficiency, despite mounting debts. Toothache added to his wretchedness, although he immortalised that particular pain in verse too, and the giggles of his children at his discomfort:

A' down my beard the slavers trickle,
I throw the wee stools o'er the mickle,
While round the fire the giglets keckle,
To see me loup,
An', raving mad, I wish a heckle
Were I' their doup!

Where'er that place be priests ca' hell,
Where a' the tones of misery yell,
An ranked plagues their numbers tell,
In dreadfu' raw,
Thou, toothache, surely bear'st the bell,
Among them a'!

Burns was not alone in his worries about money and providing for his family. Others fared even worse: 1796 saw the Meal Riots in Dumfries over a shortage of food after a poor harvest.

In September 1795 his favourite child, three-year-old Elizabeth, died. Rob and Jean had sent her to Mauchline, in the hope that a change of air would restore her: the demands of Excise work meant he could not even travel north to attend her funeral, and for two months he wrote nothing. Grief made him ill, possibly with rheumatic fever, though Dr Maxwell made a diagnosis of what he called 'flying gout'.

In his dying months, Jean was again pregnant. A young woman named Jessy Lewars came into the household to help with the nursing, and for the last time in his life, Burns fell romantically in love, scribbling notes to her on a glass tumbler since he could not reach the window. For her, he wrote *O wert thou in the cold blast*.

Or were I in the wildest waste,
So black and bare, so black and bare,
The desert were a Paradise,
If thou wert there; if thou wert there.

By the summer of 1796 Burns' physical condition was so poor – racked with pain and dosed with mercury – that even a doctor might see the man was desperately ill. Eighteenth-century medicine being what it was, the 'cure' for an illness rheumatic in nature was deemed to be the waters of the Solway Firth, and this is what Dr Maxwell recommended. Jean, Jessy and Rob thus decamped for Brow on Solway on 3 July and once again, this time to save his life, the poet sank up to his armpits in those chilly waters, which no summer sun has ever warmed.

By chance, Maria Riddell had also been ill and was recuperating nearby. They arranged to meet. 'I was struck with his appearance on entering the room. The stamp of death was imprinted on his features. He seemed already touching the brink of eternity. His first salutation was "Well, madam, have you any commands for the other world?"'

At that meeting, Burns expressed concern for his reputation after his death: he was certainly aware that his death would create some reaction and that every piece of his writing might be used against him to damage his future reputation: that letters and verses he had written with unguarded and improper freedom, and which he hoped would be ignored, would be handed about and discussed.

He returned to Dumfries unrestored, scarcely able to walk the few steps from his carriage to his front door. Seeing a fellow member of the Royal Dumfries Volunteers, he joked: 'John, don't let the Awkward Squad fire over me'. He took to his bed in the upstairs room, and died on 21 July at five in the morning. He was 37 years old.

And After

The funeral took place on 25 July, and on the same day Jean gave birth to their ninth child. Because of Burns' militia connections, he was given a military funeral. Two regiments escorted the coffin, as well as Burns' beloved Volunteers, and the body was laid to rest in St Michael's Kirkyard, Dumfries. The Dead March from *Saul* accompanied the cortege, and the Awkward Squad did indeed fire a volley over the coffin. 21 years later, on 19 September 1817, the coffin was moved to its present resting place in the Mausoleum. Members of his family are buried with him, including Jean, who survived him by 38 years, and now lies forever by his side.

Burns' funeral procession

7 – Selected Poems and Songs

Scots Wha Hae

Scots, wha hae wi' Wallace bled,
Scots, wham Bruce has often led,
Welcome to your gory bed,
Or to victorie!
Now's the day, and now's the hour;
See the front o' battle lour;
See approach proud Edward's power
Chains and slaverie!

Wha will be a traitor knave?
Wha can fill a coward's grave?
Wha sae base as be a slave?
Let him turn and flee!
Wha for Scotland's King and law,
Freedom's sword will strongly draw,
Freeman stand, or freeman fall,
Let him follow me!

By oppression's woes and pains!
By your sons in servile chains!
We will draw our dearest veins,
But they shall be free!
Lay the proud usurpers low!
Tyrants fall in every foe!
Liberty's in every blow!
Let us do or die!

Address to a Haggis

Fair fa' your honest, sonsie face,
Great chieftain o' the pudding race!
Aboon them a' ye tak your place,
Painch, tripe, or thairm:
Weel are ye wordy o' a grace
As lang's my arm.

The groaning trencher there ye fill,
Your hurdies like a distant hill,
Your pin wad help to mend a mill
In time o' need
While thro' your pores the dews distil
Like amber bead.

His knife see rustic Labour dight,
An' cut you up wi' ready sleight,
Trenching your gushing entrails bright,
Like ony ditch;
And then, O what a glorious sight,
Warm-reekin', rich!

Then, horn for horn, they stretch an' strive:
Deil tak the hindmost! on they drive,
Till a' their weel-swall'd kytes belyve,
Are bent like drums;
Then auld Guidman, maist like to rive,
'Bethankit!' hums.

Is there that owre his French *ragout*
Or *olio* that was staw a sow,
Or *fricasse* wad mak her spew
Wi' perfect sconner,
Looks down wi' sneering, scornfu' view
On sic dinner?

Poor devil! see him owre his trash,
As feckless as a wither'd rash,
His spindle shank, a guid whip-lash,
His nieve a nit;
Thro' bloody flood or field to dash,
O how unfit!

But mark the Rustic, haggis fed,
The trembling earth resounds his tread.
Clap in his walie nieve a blade,
He'll mak it whissle;
An' legs an' arms, an' heads will sned,
Like taps o' thrissle.

Ye Pow'rs wha mak mankind your care,
And dish them out their bill o' fare,
Auld Scotland wants nae skinking ware
That jaups in luggies;
But, if ye wish her grateful' prayer,
Gie her a haggis!

Red Red Rose

O my luve is like a red, red rose,
That's newly sprung in June.
O my luve is like a melodie
That's sweetly played in tune.

As fair art thou, my bonnie lass,
So deep in luve am I.
And I will luve thee still, my dear,
Till a' the seas gang dry.

Till a' the seas gang dry, my dear,
And the rocks melt wi' the sun,
And I will luve thee still, my dear,
While the sands o' life shall run.

And fare thee weel, my only luve,
And fare thee weel awhile!
And I will come again, my luve
Tho' 'twere ten thousand mile.

Auld Lang Syne

Should auld acquaintance be forgot,
And never brought to mind?
Should auld acquaintance be forgot,
And auld lang syne!

Chorus
For auld lang syne, my dear,
For auld lang syne
We'll tak a cup o' kindness yet
For auld lang syne

And surely, ye'll be your pint stoup,
And surely I'll be mine,
And we'll tak a cup o' kindness yet
For auld lang syne.

Chorus

We twa hae run about the braes,
And pou'd the gowans fine;
But we've wandered mony a weary fit
Sin' auld lang syne.

Chorus

We twa hae paidl'd in the burn,
Frae morning sun till dine;
But seas between us braid hae roar'd
Sin' auld lang syne

Chorus

And there's a hand, my trusty fiere,
And gie's a hand o' thine;
And we'll tak a richt gude-willy waught
For auld lang syne.

Chorus

Tam o' Shanter

When chapman billies leave the street,
And drouthy neibors neibors meet;
As market days are wearing late,
And folk begin to tak the gate,
While we sit bousing at the nappy,
An' getting fou and unco happy,
We think na on the lang Scots miles,
The mosses, waters, slaps and stiles,
That lie between us and our hame,
Where sits our sulky, sullen dame,
Gathering her brows like gathering storm,
Nursing her wrath to keep it warm.

This truth fand honest Tam O' Shanter,
As he frae Ayr ae night did canter:
(Auld Ayr, wham ne'er a town surpasses,
For honest men and bonie lasses)

O Tam! had'st thou but been sae wise,
As taen thy ain wife Kate's advice!
She tauld thee weel thou was a skellum,
A blethering, blustering, drunken blellum;
That frae November till October,
Ae market-day thou was na sober;
That ilka melder wi' the Miller,
Thou sat as lang as thou had siller;
That ev'ry naig was ca'd a shoe on
The Smith and thee gat roarin fou on;
That at the Lord's house, ev'n on Sunday,
Thou drank wi' Kirkton Jean till Monday;
She prophesied that late or soon,
Thou wad be found, deep drown'd in Doon,
Or catch'd wi' warlocks in the mirk,
By Alloway's auld, haunted kirk.

Ah, gentle dames! it gars me greet,
To think how mony counsels sweet,

How mony lengthen'd, sage advices,
The husband frae the wife despises!

But to our tale: — Ae market night,
Tam had got planted unco right,
Fast by an ingle, bleezing finely,
Wi' reaming swats that drank divinely;
And at his elbow, Soutar Johnie,
His ancient, trusty, drouthy crony:
Tam lo'ed him like a very brither;
They had been fou for weeks thegither.
The night drave on wi' sangs an' clatter;
And aye the ale was growing better:
The Landlady and Tam grew gracious,
Wi' favours secret, sweet and precious:
The Souter tauld his queerest stories;
The Landlord's laugh was ready chorus:
The storm without might rair and rustle,
Tam did na mind the storm a whistle.

Care, mad to see a man sae happy,
E'en drown'd himsel amang the nappy.
As bees flee hame wi' lades o' treasure,
The minutes wing'd their way wi' pleasure:
Kings may be blest, but Tam was glorious,
O'er a' the ills o' life victorious!

But pleasures are like poppies spread,
You seize the flow'r, its bloom is shed;
Or like the snow falls in the river,
A moment white — then melts for ever;
Or like the Borealis race,
That flit ere you can point their place;
Or like the Rainbow's lovely form
Evanishing amid the storm.—

Nae man can tether Time nor Tide,
The hour approaches Tam maun ride;
That hour, o' night's black arch the key-stane,

That dreary hour he mounts his beast in;
And sic a night he taks the road in,
As ne'er poor sinner was abroad in.

The wind blew as 'twad blawn its last;
The rattling showers rose on the blast;
The speedy gleams the darkness swallow'd;
Loud, deep, and lang the thunder bellow'd:
That night, a child might understand,
The deil had business on his hand.

Weel-mounted on his grey mare Meg,
A better never lifted leg,
Tam skelpit on thro' dub and mire,
Despising wind, and rain, and fire;
Whiles holding fast his gude blude bonnet,
Whiles crooning o'er some auld Scots sonnet,
Whiles glow'rin round wi' prudent cares,
Lest bogles catch him unawares;
Kirk-Alloway was drawing nigh,
Where ghaists and houlets nightly cry.

By this time he was cross the ford,
Where in the snaw the chapman smoor'd;
And past the birks and meikle stane,
Where drunken Charlie brak's neck-bane;
And thro' the whins, and by the cairn,
Where hunters fand the murder'd bairn;
And near the thorn, aboon the well,
Where Mungo's mither hang'd hersel'.
Before him Doon pours all his floods,
The doubling storm roars thro' the woods,
The lightnings flash from pole to pole,
Near and more near the thunders roll,
When, glimmering thro' the groaning trees,
Kirk-Alloway seem'd in a bleeze,
Thro' ilka bore the beams were glancing,
And loud resounded mirth and dancing.

Inspiring bold John Barleycorn!
What dangers thou canst make us scorn!
Wi' tippeny, we fear nae evil;
Wi' usquabae, we'll face the devil!
The swats sae ream'd in Tammie's noddle,
Fair play, he car'd na deils a boddle,
But Maggie stood, right sair astonish'd,
Till, by the heel and hand admonish'd,
She ventur'd forward on the light;
And, wow! Tam saw an unco sight!

Warlocks and witches in a dance:
Nae cotillon, brent new frae France,
But hornpipes, jigs, strathspeys, and reels,
Put life and mettle in their heels.
A winnock-bunker in the east,
There sat auld Nick, in shape o' beast;
A tousie tyke, black, grim, and large,
To gie them music was his charge.
He screw'd the pipes and gart them skirl,
Till roof and rafters a' did dirl.—
Coffins stood round, like open presses,
That shaw'd the Dead in their last dresses;
And (by some devilish cantraip sleight)
Each in its cauld hand held a light.
By which heroic Tam was able
To note upon the haly table,
A murderer's banes, in gibbet-airns;
Twa span-lang, wee, unchristened bairns;
A thief, new-cutted frae a rape,
Wi' his last gasp his gab did gape;
Five tomahawks, wi' blude red-rusted:
Five scimitars, wi' murder crusted;
A knife, a father's throat had mangled,
Whom his ain son of life bereft,
The grey hairs yet stack to the heft;

Wi' mair of horrible and awfu',
Which even to name wad be unlawfu'.

As Tammie glowr'd, amaz'd, and curious,
The mirth and fun grew fast and furious;
The Piper loud and louder blew,
The dancers quick and quicker flew,
They reel'd, they set, they cross'd, they cleekit,
Till ilka carlin swat and reekit,
And coost her duddies to the wark,
And linkit at it in her sark!

Now Tam, O Tam! had they been queans,
A' plump and strapping in their teens!
Their sarks, instead o' creeshie flainen,
Been snaw-white seventeen-hunder linen!–
Thir breeks o' mine, my only pair,
That aince were plush, o' guid blue hair,
I wad hae gien them off my hurdies,
For ae blink o' the bonie burdies!
But wither'd beldams, auld and droll,
Rigwoodie hags wad spean a foal,
Louping an' flinging on a crummock,
I wonder did na turn thy stomach.

But Tam kent what was what fu' brawlie:
There was ae winsome wench and waulie
That night enlisted in the core,
Lang after ken'd on Carrick shore
(For mony a beast to dead she shot,
And perish'd mony a bonie boat,
And shook baith meikle corn and bear,
And kept the country-side in fear);
Her cutty sark, o' Paisley harn,
That while a lassie she had worn,
In longitude tho' sorely scanty,
It was her best, and she was vauntie.
Ah! little ken'd thy reverend grannie,

That sark she coft for her wee Nannie,
Wi' twa pund Scots ('twas a' her riches),
Wad ever grac'd a dance of witches!

But here my Muse her wing maun cour,
Sic flights are far beyond her power;
To sing how Nannie lap and flang
(A souple jade she was and strang),
And how Tam stood, like ane bewitch'd,
And thought his very een enrich'd:
Even Satan glowr'd, and fidg'd fu' fain,
And hotch'd and blew wi' might and main:
Till first ae caper, syne anither,
Tam tint his reason a' thegither,
And roars out, "Weel done, Cutty-sark!"
And in an instant all was dark:
And scarcely had he Maggie rallied,
When out the hellish legion sallied.

As bees bizz out wi' angry fyke,
When plundering herds assail their byke;
As open pussie's mortal foes,
When, pop! she starts before their nose;
As eager runs the market-crowd,
When "Catch the thief!" resounds aloud;
So Maggie runs, the witches follow,
Wi' mony an eldritch skreich and hollo.

Ah, Tam! Ah, Tam! thou'll get thy fairin!
In hell they'll roast thee like a herrin!
In vain thy Kate awaits thy comin!
Kate soon will be a woefu' woman!
Now, do thy speedy utmost, Meg,
And win the key-stane o' the brig;
There, at them thou thy tail may toss,
A running stream they dare na cross.
But ere the key-stane she could make,
The fient a tail she had to shake!

For Nannie, far before the rest,
Hard upon noble Maggie prest,
And flew at Tam wi' furious ettle;
But little wist she Maggie's mettle!
Ae spring brought off her master hale,
But left behind her ain grey tail:
The carlin claught her by the rump,
And left poor Maggie scarce a stump.

Now, wha this tale o' truth shall read,
Ilk man, and mother's son, take heed:
Whene'er to Drink you are inclin'd,
Or Cutty-sarks rin in your mind,
Think ye may buy the joys o'er dear;
Remember Tam o' Shanter's mare.

Plate M.

Ae Fond Kiss

Ae fond kiss and then we sever
Ae fareweel, alas, for ever!
Deep in heart-wrung tears I'll pledge thee,
Warring sighs and groans I'll wage thee.
Who shall say that fortune grieves him,
While the star of hope she leaves him?
Me, nae cheerfu' twinkle lights me:
Dark despair around benights me.

I'll ne'er blame my partial fancy,
Nae thing could resist my Nancy!
But to see her was to love her;
Love but her, and love for ever.
Had we never lov'd sae kindly,
Had we never lov'd sae blindly,
Never met or never parted
We had ne'er been broken hearted.

Fare thee weel, thou first and fairest,
Fare thee weel, thou best and dearest,
Thine be ilka joy and treasure,
Peace, enjoyment, love and pleasure.
Ae fond kiss, and then we sever;
Ae fareweel, alas, for ever!
Deep in heart-wrung tears I'll pledge thee,
Warring sighs and groans I'll wage thee!

8 – The Poems and Songs

'I don't know if you have a just idea of my character, but I wish you to
see me as I am. I am, as most people of my trade are, a strange will o'
the wisp being; the victim too frequently of much imprudence and
many follies – My great constituent elements are Pride and Passion: the
first I have endeavoured to humanize into integrity and honour; the last
makes me a Devotee to the warmest degree of enthusiasm, in Love,
Religion, or Friendship...'

The exact status of Robert Burns in the pantheon of world poets may be
open to debate: poetry is, after all, a very subjective passion. But few poets
have been – or are – so well-loved, not only in his own country where he
remains forever 'Caledonia's Bard', but beyond. *Auld Lang Syne* is the most-
often sung song in the world – even though few know more than the first
verse, and usually get that wrong.

His poems have been translated into over 25 languages, including
Russian and Japanese. One of the earliest biographies of Burns was published
by the Frenchman Auguste Angellier in 1893. Its two volumes are *La Vie*
and *Les Oeuvres* – even then recognizing that his life was as fascinating as
his work.

Burns' output was prodigious, even though his life as a published poet
barely covered a decade: the Kilmarnock Edition came out in 1786, and ten
years later he was dead. Nor was he ever that privileged person, the full-
time writer. All his writing was done in parallel with other, demanding
occupations, first as a farmer and then as a farmer and exciseman, when a
day's work would end with reports to be written and accounts to be entered.

Burns composed mostly out of doors, in his head – although he always
carried a pen and ink with him, to scribble down ideas. The rhymes sprang
in him as from a deep well. He also wrote for the fun of it: for his friends, for
the people he met and drank with – often, he would write a poem and
then give it away at once. As he wrote, he was eager to share, and to read
aloud. His great gift was for lyric poetry. His passion for 'mending' songs
has already been mentioned, but an ear for music, and the lilt of a hidden
melody, runs like a shining thread through the best of his poetry. In Burns,
the terms 'poem' and 'song' can be virtually interchangeable. Burns gives
this description of himself in the act of composition:

'My way is: I consider the poetic Sentiment, correspondent to my idea of the musical expression; then chuse my theme; begin one Stanza; when that is composed, which is generally the most difficult part of the business, I walk out, sit down now & then, look out for objects in Nature around me that are in unison or harmony with the cogitations of my fancy & workings of my bosom; humming every now & then the air with the verses I have framed: when I feel my Muse beginning to jade, I retire to the solitary fireside of my study, & there commit my effusions to paper; swinging, at intervals, on the hind-legs of my elbow-chair, by way of calling forth my own critical strictures, as my pen goes on. – Seriously, this, at home, is almost invariably my way. – What damn'd Egotism!'

Jean Armour later gave a description of her husband's domestic life and habits at home in Dumfries: '... he was always reading ... At all meals he had a book beside him on the table.' She also describes him writing: 'When at home in the evening, he employed his time in writing and reading, with the children playing about him. Their prattle never disturbed him.'

The Complete Illustrated Poems, Songs and Ballads of Robert Burns contains over 500 titles together with a comprehensive glossary. The latter is invaluable for those who feel that a major obstacle to reading Burns' poetry is the Scots tongue in which he wrote – his own native, unvarnished speech. While some words are undoubtedly incomprehensible without an accompanying glossary, this resistance can often be overcome simply by reading the poem aloud and enjoying the sound and the rhythm of the words.

Burns wrote on many topics: when anything interested, engaged or angered him, he wrote a poem about it, though the underlying themes of his work are consistent – for example, personal integrity and the value of the individual more than his station in life. An example of this variety – though hardly his greatest poem – is the *Address to a Haggis:* a piece of tongue-in-cheek jauntiness, in honour of that traditional Scots dish of sheep's stomach and spices which is now the culinary cornerstone of every Burns Supper.

Fair fa' your honest, sonsie face,
Great chieftain o' the pudding-race!
Aboon them a' ye tak your place,
Pinch, tripe, or thairm:
Weel are ye wordy o' a grace
As lang's my arm.

Typically, the poem moves from everyday observation to philosophical point: let other nations enjoy their rich and over-rich foods, the haggis-fed Scot grows sturdy on this honest fare: 'Auld Scotland wants nae skinking ware/That jaups in luggies.'

Extracts have been selected here from a few of Burns' best-known poems and the subject matter that warmed him: love, politics, animals, hypocrisy, religion and the supernatural.

One of the first poems Burns wrote, and recited to his pleasantly astonished brother Gilbert, was *The Death and Dying Words of Poor Mailie*. Poor Mailie was a pet sheep. In fact Mailie had merely become entangled in her tether and rolled over, and Rob was able to set her upright, but he was inspired to compose a sentimental verse in which Mailie gives a dying blessing to her twin lambs. The poem includes a verse in which the good farmer – Burns himself, of course – came in for this pat on the back:

> Tell him, he was a Master kind;
> And aye was good to me and mine;
> And now my dying charge I give him,
> My helpless lambs, I trust them with him.

The evidence is that Burns *was* a Master kind, both to servants and to animals. All farmers have a relationship with their animals, of course, based on commercial value if nothing else – in the eighteenth century, when animals were killed only for food in old age or on special occasions, this was especially true. The family's provision of milk, cheese, butter and wool came directly from their own animals, and the health and wellbeing of these creatures was paramount.

But Burns seems to have had a genuine attachment to animals: lambs became pets, there was usually a dog trotting at his heels, and one of the few occasions on which he lost his temper with a farm-worker was when the man did not cut the potatoes small enough, and Burns was frantic that the beasts might choke on them.

In a letter written in 1789, he describes seeing a hare shot, but not killed, and dragging itself away to die. 'There is something in all that multiform business of destroying, for our sport, individuals in the animal creation that do not injure us materially that I could never reconcile to my ideas of native Virtue and Eternal Right,' he wrote in prose. But in poetry:

> Seek, mangled wretch, some place of wonted rest,
> No more of rest, but now thy dying bed!
> The sheltering rushes whistling o'er thy head,
> The cold earth with thy bloody bosom prest.

His collie Luath achieved posthumous fame as one of the protagonists in *The Twa' Dogs*, a political fable about the difference between rich and poor. Horses owned at various times, Pegasus and Maggie, feature in other poems. In *The Auld Farmer's New-Year Morning Salutation to his Auld Mare, Maggie*, Burns pays warm tribute to the companionship animals provide down the years: horse and rider have enjoyed the seasons together, and now

> We've worn to crazy years thegither;
> We'll toyte about wi' ane anither;
> Wi' tentie care I'll flit thy tether
> To some hain'd rig,
> Whare ye may nobly rax your leather,
> Wi' sma' fatigue.

In poetry the plight of animals can be a metaphor for the human condition, and Burns' two most famous animal poems take as their subjects not farm or domestic animals, but vermin. *To a Mouse* is rich in compassion for the suffering of a helpless, panic-stricken creature. The explanation underneath the title is: *On Turning Her Up in Her Nest with the Plough, November 1785*.

> Wee, sleekit, cowrin, tim-rous beastie,
> Oh, what a panic's in thy breastie!
> Thou need na start awa sae hasty,
> Wi' bickering brattle!
> I wad be laith to rin an' chase thee,
> Wi' murd'ring prattle!
>
> I'm truly sorry man's dominion,
> Has broken nature's social union,
> An justifies that ill opinion,
> Which makes thee startle
> At me, thy poor, earth-born companion,
> An fellow-mortal!

The final stanzas gives an insight into Burns himself. His compassion for animals is tempered by the belief that as their lives are lived only in the present moment, so is their pain. The suffering of humans is greater because it can cast its shadow backwards and forwards:

> But Mousie, thou art no they lane,
> In proving foresight may be vain;
> The best-laid schemes o' mice an' men
> Gang aft agley,
> An' leave us nought but grief an' pain,
> For promised joy!
>
> Still thou art blest, compar'd wi' me;
> The present only toucheth thee:
> But och! I backward cast my e'e,
> On prospects drear!
> An' forward, tho' I canna see,
> I guess an' fear!

To A Louse was written *On Seeing one on a Lady's Bonnet in Church*. It is unknown whether Burns drew her attention to this visitor. Again, the poem moves from general observation to a universal insight:

> O wad some Power the giftie gie us
> To see oursels as ithers see us!
> It wad frae mony a blunder free us,
> An' foolish notion!
> What airs in dress and gait wad lea'e us,
> An' ev'n devotion!

Self-knowledge, lack of pretence, an understanding and acceptance of who and what one is – these themes preoccupied Burns, a poor man who felt himself the equal of an earl or a blacksmith, and who knew that only the mercy of God kept him from the destitution he saw around him.

Religion – or, more accurately, the church – was the theme of two fine poems, *The Unco Guid* – subtitled *Or the Rigidly Righteous* – and *Holy Willie's Prayer*.

All his life, Burns attended church twice on Sundays and faithfully observed the Presbyterian religion of his father. Privately, though, he railed against the power, the hypocrisy and the rigidity of the kirk. His sexual misbehaviour brought him into direct confrontation with the clergy and, after the custom of the time, he was obliged to undergo public humiliation in church for his 'seduction' of Jean Armour, but Burns' quarrel with religious observance went deeper than this. It sprang from a personal feeling that religion should be a natural, joyous and spontaneous feeling, expressed through life and the delights of life – love, music and song – and not confined within the straitjacket of supposedly moral behaviour. A letter written in 1789 contrasts Burns' natural piety with that of the kirk:

> 'The first Sunday of May; a breezy blue-skyed noon some time about the beginning, and a hoary morning & a calm sunny day about the end, of Autumn; these, time out of mind, have been with me a kind of Holidays. [Holy Days]. – Not like the Sacramental, Executioner-face of a Kilmarnock Communion; but to laugh or cry, be chearful or pensive, moral, or devout, according to the mood & tense of the Season & myself.'

The Unco Guid echoes the New Testament quotation: 'Let him who is without sin cast the first stone'. Burns suspects not that the righteous are in fact better than others whose faults and folly they love to 'mark and tell', but simply better at hiding their own follies. The poem is a plea for understanding of others, and silence on the subject of their faults: we cannot know the secrets of another's heart, or what has led them to act as they have. Ours is not to judge or condemn, for this belongs to God alone.

> Then gently scan your brother man,
> Still gentler sister woman;
> Tho' they may gang a kennin wrang,
> To step aside is human;
> One point must still be greatly dark, -
> The moving Why they do it;
> And just as lamely can ye mark,
> How far perhaps they rue it.
>
> Who made the heart, 'tis He alone
> Decidely can try us;
> He knows each chord, its various tone,
> Each spring, its various bias:
> Then at the balance let's be mute,
> We never can adjust it;
> What's done we partly may compute,
> But know not what's resisted.

Holy Willie's Prayer is a mischievous satire on the self-righteous. 'Holy Willie' was one William Fisher, a man who undertook his Christian duties with zeal and energy but without any sense of genuine warmth. At Fisher's behest the minister and kirk session at Mauchline condemned Gavin Hamilton, Burns' friend, for failing to observe the Sabbath in the proper manner. Outraged on his friend's behalf, Burns portrayed Holy Willie's humbug and cant in verse. Fisher himself later fell foul of the kirk session, and stood before the elders to receive a public rebuke for drunkenness. For posterity, Holy Willie is recorded as a man glad he is not as others are:

> O Lord, Thou kens what zeal I bear,
> When drinkers drink, an' swearers swear,
> An' singing here, an' dancing there,
> Wi' great and sma',
> For I am keepit by Thy fear
> Free frae them a'.

The equality of man is a theme often returned to, but nowhere more famously than in the poem *A Man's A Man*. This is the most uncompromising lyric insisting on the fundamental rightness of the egalitarian ethic which, in Burns' lifetime, fuelled the American and the French revolutions. Never mind a man's parentage, or inherited wealth, or luck – what counts in the man 'of independent mind', who mocks such 'tinsel show'.

> The rank is but the guinea's stamp,
> The man's the gowd for a' that.

> Then let us pray that come it may,
> (As come it will for a' that)
> That Sense and Worth, o'er a' the earth,
> Shall bear the gree, an' a' that.
> For a' that, an' a' that,
> It's coming yet for a' that,
> That man to man, the world o'er,
> Shall brithers be for a' that.

Burns' sense of present injustice was allied with a romantic sense of the past, and a passionate love of the healing powers of the Scottish land he inhabited. He was a Jacobite out of a sense of romance more than anything else – as a political cause, it was long since dead, and the Bonnie Prince described in *Charlie, He's My Darling* was in reality a dying man in alcoholic exile:

'Twas on a Monday morning,
Right early in the year,
That Charlie came to our town,
The young Chevalier.

There is a wonderfully singable chorus:

An' Charlie, he's my darling,
My darling, my darling,
Charlie he's my darling,
The young Chevalier.

That earlier period of Scottish history when Scots fought to establish an independent, united kingdom free of English domination was the subject of *Scots Wha Hae*, dedicated to William Wallace, the hero whom Burns would have followed without question.

Scots, wha hae wi' Wallace bled,
Scots, wham Bruce has aften led,
Welcome to your gorie bed,
Or to victorie!

Wallace embodied qualities Burns saw as uniquely Scots: fierce pride allied to loyalty to a noble cause. In *The Author's Cry and Prayer* – a satire on the London government's taxation of Scotch whisky – he wrote:

Auld Scotland has a raucle tongue;
She's just a devil wi' a rung;
An' if she promise auld or young
To tak' their part,
Tho' by the neck she should be strung,
She'll no desert.

The drudgery and disappointments of a farming life never dimmed Burns' passion for the land. In song, that passion could be unfocused and generalised as in *My Heart's in the Highlands*:

My heart's in the Highlands, my heart is not here;
My heart's in the Highlands, a-chasing the deer;
A-chasing the wild deer, and following the roe,
My heart's in the Highlands wherever I go.

With a place he knew well, the verse has a focus, but the lyricism is just as eloquent. Burns is said to have loved the sound of running water, and here the verse flows as effortlessly as the crystal waters of the *Sweet Afton* itself:

> Flow gently, sweet Afton! among thy green braes
> Flow gently, I'll sing thee a song in thy praise;
> My Mary's asleep by thy murmuring stream,
> Flow gently, sweet Afton, disturb not her dream.
>
> Thou stock dove whose echo resounds thro' the glen,
> Ye wild whistling blackbirds in yon thorny den,
> Thou green crested lapwing, thy screaming forbear,
> I charge you, disturb not my slumbering Fair.

Burns is chiefly, though inaccurately, remembered as the poet and lyricist of love. The index of his Collected Poems is liberally sprinkled with the names of 'rapture-giving' women to whom he dedicated poems – Mary, Clarinda, Jeanie, Peggy, as well as the anonymous yearnings of *I Love my Love in Secret* or *The Lass that Made the Bed to Me*.

Love is the obvious subject for song and verse: the more unhappy, the less requited, the greater the doom of that love, the meatier the verse is likely to be. A writer can only, after all, write well about what occupies him most – and it can be argued that Burns was more in love with love itself than necessarily with the individual women about whom he wrote. Their names at the top of the poems were virtually interchangeable – and in fact, he is known to have done this when his affections shifted in mid-composition. Real women are not being described in these poems: they are objects of love and yearning, and thus universal. For example the sentiments expressed in *A Red, Red Rose*:

> O my love is like a red, red rose,
> That's newly sprung in June;
> O my love is like the melody,
> That's sweetly played in tune
>
> As fair thou art, my bonny lass,
> So deep in love am I,
> And I will love thee still, my dear,
> Till all the seas gang dry.

It's the all-or-nothing passion that occupies the poet here, not the grit of any authentic attachment. The most bittersweet – and the best – of his love poems was written about a real event: *Ae Fond Kiss* was composed by Burns after his final parting from 'Clarinda' – Agnes McLehose:

> Ae fond kiss, and then we sever;
> Ae farewell, and then forever!
> Deep in heart-wrung tears I'll pledge thee,
> Warring sighs and groans I'll wage thee.
> Who shall say that Fortune grieves him,
> While the star of hope she leaves him?
> Me, nae cheerful twinkle lights me;
> Dark despair around benights me.
>
> I'll ne'er blame my partial fancy,
> Nothing could resist my Nancy:
> But to see her was to love her;
> Love but her, and love for ever.
> Had we never lov'd sae kindly,
> Had we never lov'd sae blindly,
> Never met – or never parted,
> We had ne'er been broken-hearted.

Many of Burns' love poems are as light and inconsequential as candy floss: but there is a genuine heart-rending quality to this one which transcends all the others – by any standards, it is a great poem.

Not all Burns' love poetry was written from the perspective of pure love-from-afar. A robust enthusiasm for the joys of houghmagandie – fornication – pervades a pleasing number of them. *The Holy Fair* is a jolly account of a country fair and chance encounters:

> How many hearts this day converts
> O' sinners and o' lasses!
> Their hearts o' stane, gin night, are gane
> As saft as ony flesh is;
> There's some are fou o' love divine;
> There's some are fou o' brandy;
> An' many jobs that day begin,
> May end in houghmagandie
> Some ither day.

John Anderson, my Jo, is a tender song about a love which has weathered the years and survives happily in the warm richness of married affection:

> John Anderson, my Jo,
> When we were first acquent,

Your locks were like the raven,
Your bonie brow was brent;
But now your brow is beld, John,
Your locks are like the snow;
But blessings on your frosty pow,
John Anderson, my Jo

John Anderson, my jo, John,
We clamb the hill thegither;
And mony a cantie day, John,
We've had wi' ane anither:
Now we maun totter down, John,
And hand in hand we'll go,
And sleep thegither at the foot,
John Anderson, my jo.

An earlier version, attributed to Burns, is raunchier by far but none the less
tender:

John Anderson, my jo, John,
When first that ye began,
Ye had as good a tail-tree,
As ony ither man;
But now its waxen wan, John,
And wrinkles to and fro;
I've twa gae-ups for ae gae-down,
John Anderson, my jo.

When we come on before, John,
See that ye do your best;
When ye begin to haud me,
See that ye grip me fast;
See that ye grip me fast, John,
Until that I cry 'Oh!'
Your back shall crack or I do that,
John Anderson, my jo.

The Cotter's Saturday Night

Two longer poems of Burns deserve special mention. *The Cotter's Saturday Night* is a poem of hearth and home, specifically, that idealized hearth and home Burns knew best: the one-room cottage, the but-and-ben of the farm

The Cotter's Saturday Night

labourer. The gentle 'toil-worn' Cotter himself is a portrait of William Burnes, Rob's father, coming home on a Saturday night, his week's work over:

> At length his lonely cot appears in view,
> beneath the shelter of an aged tree;
> Th' expectant wee-things, toddlin, stacher through
> To meet their dad, wi' flichterin noise and glee.
> His wee bit ingle, blinkin bonilie,
> His clean hearth-stane, his thrifty wifie's smile,
> The lisping infant, prattling on his knee,
> Does a' his weary kiaugh and care beguile,
> And makes him quite forget his labour and his toil.

A newcomer joins this loving domestic circle – for Jenny, the eldest, has brought a young man home for parental approval. The strapping lad is welcomed – the mother well-pleased he is no 'wild, worthless rake'. The boy shares the frugal supper of porridge before the cotter takes down the family bible and 'Let us worship God!' he says with solemn air.

It is an idealized portrait painted in the sombre hues of a seventeenth-century Dutch Master, a serene domestic interior depicting simple people in simple activities, content with themselves and with each other. And this is the Scotland, and the life, which the poet cherishes most:

O Scotia! my dear, my native soil!
For whom my warmest wish to Heaven is sent,
Long may thy hardy sons of rustic toil
Be blest with health, and peace, and sweet content!
And O! may Heaven their simple lives prevent
From luxury's contagion, weak and vile!
Then, howe'er crowns and coronets be rent,
A virtuous populace may rise the while,
And stand a wall of fire around their much-lov'd isle.

From the calm still-life of *The Cotter's Saturday Night*, it is a scary helter-skelter ride into the paranormal nightmare of *Tam o' Shanter*.

Clay figures – Souter Johnnie's Cottage

Tam o' Shanter

The Presbyterian kirk represented the official, sanctioned beliefs and laws of eighteenth-century Scotland: superstition and magic the unofficial underbelly of belief. Scotland was, after all, the European country which had burnt the highest proportion of its female population as witches – a practice that had only ended at the beginning of the century in which Burns was born.

The tendency to see the hand of a malign fate or person behind the accidents of everyday country life – a cow that dies, a crop that fails, a blight, a sick child that fails to thrive – is strong. As a child, Burns was horrified and fascinated by the tales told to him and his siblings by one Betty Davidson, a cousin of his mother's. When Betty came to stay she brought with her what Burns later described as 'the largest collection in the country of tales and songs concerning devils, ghosts, fairies, brownies, witches, warlocks, spunkies, kelpies, elf-candles, dead-lights, wraiths, apparitions, cantraips, enchanted towers, giants, dragons, and other trumpery.' The children could not get enough of them.

The tale begins in the town of Ayr, on market day.

Auld Ayr, wham ne'er a town surpasses
For honest men and bonie lasses

Tam – convivial chap – has, perhaps understandably, ignored the advice of his wife Kate – a 'sulky, sullen dame ... nursing her wrath to keep it warm'. Instead of riding straight home after market, he has been succumbing to a common temptation in the pub: 'Thou sat as long as thou had siller [silver].'

The tavern was warm and comforting, and Tam's companion, Souter Johnnie, a trusty pal: as Burns remarks, they loved each other as only those who get very drunk together can.

But pleasures are like poppies spread,
You seize the flow'r, its bloom is shed;
Or like the snow falls in the river,
A moment white – then melts for ever ...

Nae man can tether Time nor Tide,
The hour approaches Tam maun ride;
That hour, o' night's black arch the key-stane,
That dreary hour he mounts his beast in;
And sic a night he taks the road in,
As ne'er poor sinner was abroad in.

Mounting his grey mare Meg, Tam leaves the nest-like snug of the inn and sets his face homeward. The reader feels the prick of suspense as Tam nears old Alloway Kirk – the area itself is soaked in past horror:

> And thro' the whins, and by the cairn,
> Where hunters fand the murder'd bairn;
> And near the thorn, aboon the well,
> Where Mungo's mither hang'd hersel'.

Maggie was alert to the dangers before Tam himself: inspired by whisky, he felt he could face the devil – which is, in fact, what he was soon to do. For

Alloway Kirkyard

the kirkyard held an 'unco sight. Warlocks and witches in a dance' – a hellish coterie of ghostly malevolent beings at play, there before him.

In a letter recounting the prose version of the poem, Burns wrote: '... a dance of witches merrily footing it round their old sooty blackguard master, who was keeping them all alive with the power of the bagpipe ... How the gentleman was dressed, tradition does not say; but the ladies were all in their smocks; and one of them happening unluckily to have a smock which was considerably too short to answer all the purpose of that piece of dress ...' The traditional name for this garment was a cutty-sark, and Tam is discovered on account of his fascination with the fetchingly garbed wench: he roars out 'Weel done, Cutty-sark!' in spite of himself

And in an instant all was dark:
And scarcely had he Maggie rallied,
When out the hellish legion sallied.

As bees bizz out wi' angry fyke,
When plundering herds assail their byke;
As open pussie's mortal foes,
When, pop! she starts before their nose;
As eager runs the market-crowd,
When 'Catch the thief!' resounds aloud;
So Maggie runs, the witches follow,
Wi' mony an eldritch skreich and hollo

Tam is literally hag-ridden home in a headlong and terrifying ride. It is the Brig o' Doon that can save them – for as everyone knows, 'A running stream they dare na cross.' They very nearly do not make it: Tam is saved by the supreme efforts of his old mare, whose tail is sacrificed – for Nannie, the one with the cutty sark, grabs hold of Maggie's tail and pulls it off. Burns again: '... To the last hours of the noble creature's life, [her taillessness was] an awful warning to the Carrick farmers, not to stay too late in Ayr markets.' This thrilling tale ends, as all should, with a suitably moral warning:

Now, wha this tale o' truth shall read,
Ilk man, and mother's son, take heed:
Whene'er to Drink you are inclin'd,
Or Cutty-sarks rin in your mind,
Think ye may buy the joys o'er dear,
Remember Tam o' Shanter's mare.

Old Brig o' Doon

It is a superb poem, a vigorous sustained narrative, written in the Scots language of bed, plough and pub, and accessible to all. It is Burns' greatest accomplishment, and he knew it.

Map 3: Places to Visit

1 Alloway Old Kirk
2 Bachelors' Club, Tarbolton
3 Blair Castle
4 Brig o' Doon, Alloway
5 Burns Club and Museum, Irvine
6 Burns Cottage and Museum, Alloway
7 Burns House, Dumfries
8 Burns Monument and Gardens, Alloway
9 Burns' House Museum and Mauchline
  Kirkyard, Mauchline
10 Canongate Cemetery, Edinburgh
11 Dean Castle, Kilmarnock
12 Ellisland Farm

13 Georgian House, Edinburgh
14 Gladstone's Land, Edinburgh
15 Glasgow Vennel, Irvine
16 Globe Inn, Dumfries
17 National Burns Memorial Tower, Mauchline
18 Poosie Nansies Inn, Mauchline
19 Robert Burns Centre, Dumfries
20 Scottish National Portrait Gallery, Edinburgh
21 Souter Johnnies Cottage, Kirkoswald
22 St Michael's Kirkyard, Dumfries
23 Tam o' Shanter Experience, Alloway
24 Writers' Museum, Edinburgh

•3

• Dundee

SCOTLAND   Perth•

• Stirling

Edinburgh• 10,13,14,20,24

•Glasgow

•5,15 •11
    •2 •9,17,18
Ayr
•1,4,6,8,23

•21

12
Dumfries •7,16,19,22

ENGLAND

Places to Visit

P Parking
S Sales Area
Refreshments
WC Toilet
£ Admission Charge
♿ Disabled
NTS National Trust for Scot.
(www.nts.org.uk/www.scotlandforyou.co.uk)

1 Alloway Old Kirk

Off A719, Alloway, Ayrshire (Burns National Heritage Park)

The ruin of this old church is where Tam o' Shanter saw the dancing witches. William Burnes, Burns' father, is buried here. The ruin and kirkyard have recently been conserved and repaired, and they reopened in 2008.

Open all year

2 Bachelors' Club

Off A758, 7.5 miles NE of Ayr, Tarbolton, Ayrshire (NTS)

The upstairs room in which Robert Burns was initiated into Freemasonry, attended dancing classes and helped found the Bachelors' Club debating society is furnished with period items and contains mementoes of the poet.

☎ 01292 541940—Open Easter or Apr-Oct, Fri-Tue 13.00-17.00.

P S £

3 Blair Castle

Off B8079, 1 mile NW of Blair Atholl, Perthshire

Blair Castle, which dates from the 13th century, is an impressive castle and mansion set in acres of park land. Home to the Dukes of Atholl for nearly 800 years. Many rooms to visit. Collections of paintings, arms, armour, china, costumes and Jacobite mementoes. Garden.

www.blair-castle.co.uk

☎ 01796 481207—Open Apr-Oct, daily; Nov-Dec, Tue & Sat only

P S WC £ ♿ Limited fac's

4 Brig o' Doon

Alloway, Ayrshire (Burns National Heritage Park)

This old bridge, which crosses the River Doon in a single span, is featured in *Tam o' Shanter*, and is where Tam at last escapes from the witches.

Open all year

5 Burns Club and Museum, Irvine

Off A737, Eglinton Street, Irvine, Ayrshire

The Burns Club was founded in 1826 by friends of Robert Burns. Its museum contains manuscripts of the first edition of the poems and other mementoes of his life.

www.irvineburnsclub.org

☎ 01294 204253—Open Summer Mon, Wed, Fri & Sat 14.30-16.30; winter Sat 14.30-16.30; tel to confirm

P WC

6 Burns Cottage and Museum, Alloway

Off B7024, Alloway, Ayrshire (Burns National Heritage Park)

Robert Burns was born in the cottage that his father built in 1759, and the building has been completely renovated and contains many mementoes and manuscripts belonging to Scotland's favourite poet; there is also an audio-visual presentation.

www.burnsheritagepark.com

☎ 01292 441215—Open all year,

daily: Apr-Sep 10.00-17.30, Oct-Mar 10.00-17.00; Tearoom, Jun-Sep.

P 🍽 S wc £ & Access

7 Burns House, Dumfries

Off A766, Burns Street, Dumfries

Robert Burns lived in this house with his family from May 1793 until his death in 1796. Furnishings are of the period and many mementoes of the poet are on display. One of the windows has his name scratched on it by his diamond ring.

www.dumgal.gov.uk/museums

📞 01387 255297—Open Apr-Sep, daily 10.00-17.00, Sun PM; Oct-Mar, Tue-Sat, closed 13.00-14.00

P Nearby S wc Nearby & Lim

8 Burns Monument and Gardens, Alloway

Off A719, Alloway
(Burns National Heritage Park)

The Grecian monument to Burns was built in 1823, and there are fine garden walks and statues of characters from his poems housed in a small museum.

📞 01292 443700—Open all year

9 Burns House Museum & Kirkyard, Mauchline

Off A716, town centre, Mauchline, Ayrshire

Robert Burns once lived in this house. The museum features traditional and interactive exhibits about, and artefacts belonging, to Burns. Refurbished in 2004, there is an informative audio-visual presentation. Disabled toilets.

A number of Burns' contemporaries are buried in Mauchline Kirkyard, opposite the museum, including 'Holy Willie', Gavin Hamilton and 'Poosie Nansie', as well as three of Burns' young daughters.

www.visiteastayrshire.com
www.mauchlinevillage.co.uk

📞 01290 550045—Open May-Sep, Tue-Sat 10.00-16.00; telephone to confirm

P Nearby S wc £

10 Canongate Cemetery

Canongate, up from Holyrood Palace, Edinburgh

The burial place of Robert Fergusson, who died in 1774; and Mrs Agnes McLehose, 'Clarinda'. David Rizzio and Adam Smith are also buried here.

www.canongatekirk.org.uk

Access at all reasonable times

11 Dean Castle

Off B7038, 1 mile NE of Kilmarnock, Ayrshire

Fine restored castle, dating from the 14th century, and held by the Boyd family for 400 years. Park. Museum housing collections of armour and musical instruments. The castle is also home to a copy of the *Kilmarnock Edition* of Burns' work.

www.deancastle.com

📞 01563 522702—Open Mar-Sep 11.00-17.00, Oct-Feb 10.00-16.00

P 🍽 S wc £ & Limited access

12 Ellisland Farm

Off A76, 6 miles N of Dumfries

The home of Robert Burns from 1788-91. Recently restored with new displays, audio-visual presentation and attractive riverside walks.

www.ellislandfarm.co.uk

📞 01387 740426—Open Apr-Sep, Mon-Sat 10.00-17.00, closed 13.00-14.00, Sun 14.00-17.00; Oct- Mar, Tue- Sat 14.00-17.00

P £

13 Georgian House

Charlotte Square, Edinburgh (NTS)
Built by Robert Adam, the Georgian House dates from the 18th century and is a fine example of architecture of the New Town of Edinburgh. Audio-visual programme.

☎ 0131 225 2160—Open Mar-Nov, daily: times vary depending on season: confirm by phone or web if necessary.

🅿 Nearby 🖳 Ⓢ ♿ 🚻 Facilities

14 Gladstone's Land

Lawnmarket (near top of Royal Mile), Edinburgh (NTS)
A typical 17th-century tenement of the Old Town of Edinburgh. The house has original painted ceilings, as well as a reconstructed shop.

☎ 0131 226 5856—Open Easter-Oct, daily 10.00-17.00; Jul & Aug 10.00-19.00

Ⓢ ♿ Facilities

15 Glasgow Vennel, Irvine

Off A737, Irvine, Ayrshire
The thatched shop where Robert Burns learnt to dress flax still survives but the Glasgow Vennel Museum which was housed here has closed and the building is now used as a local and family history centre. Some of the exhibits are in the Burns Club (see that entry on page 79).

16 Globe Inn

Off A756, Globe Inn Close, Dumfries
A fine hostelry since 1610, Burns visited this pub often. Some fine 18th-century panelling and the bedroom he used has been preserved. Said to be haunted by the ghost of Helen Park, who had a daughter by Robert Burns.
www.globeinndumfries.co.uk

☎ 01387 252335—Public House

17 National Burns Memorial Tower, Mauchline

Off A76, Mauchline, Ayrshire
Opened in 1896 as a memorial to Robert Burns, there is an interpretation centre

Robert Burns Centre, Dumfries

on the upper floors depicting the life of Robert Burns in Mauchline.

Access at all reasonable times– view from exterior

18 Poosie Nansies Inn

Off A76, Mauchline, Ayrshire

This inn was frequented by Burns, and was run by Nancy and Geordie Gibson.

☎ 01290 550316—Public house

19 Robert Burns Centre, Dumfries

Off A756, Mill Road, in Dumfries town centre

A museum about Robert Burns, with an audio-visual interpretation and exhibition about Scotland's most popular poet, as well as many other items connected with Burns. www.dumgal.gov.uk/museums

☎ 01387 264808—Open daily Apr-Sep; open Oct-Mar, Tue-Sat

P 💷 S WC & & WC; ramped access; lift to 1st floor

20 Scottish National Portrait Gallery

Queen Street, Edinburgh

The gallery contains portraits of many famous Scots, including Robert Burns, as well as Mary, Queen of Scots, many Jacobites, David Hume, Walter Scott and others. Artists include Raeburn, Reynolds, Gainsborough and Rodin. www.nationalgalleries.org

☎ 0131 556 8921—Open all year, daily except 25 & 26 Dec

P Nearby 💷 S WC & Facilities

21 Souter Johnnies Cottage, Kirkoswald

Off A77, 4 miles W of Maybole, Ayrshire

(NTS)

The home of John Davidson, the 'souter' – cobbler – in Burns' poem *Tam o' Shanter*, this thatched cottage features mementoes of Burns as well as tools and exhibits of the cobbler's craft. There is

Souter Johnnie's Cottage, Kirkoswald

Writers' Museum, Lady Stair's Close, Edinburgh

also a cottage garden and life-sized statues dating from the 1830s.

☎ 01655 760603—Open Apr-Sep, Fri-Tue 11.30-17.00

[P] Nearby [S]

22 St Michael's Kirkyard, Dumfries

Off A756, Corner of St Michael Street and Brooms Road, Dumfries
The final resting place – in a large Grecian mausoleum – of Burns, who died in 1796, as well as his wife, Jean Armour, and six of their children. The church is also often open – Burns had a family pew here.

stmichaelschurchdumfries.org
Access at all reasonable times

23 Tam o' Shanter Experience, Alloway

Murdoch's Lane, Alloway (Burns National Heritage Park)
This museum features an audio-visual presentation – using all the latest multimedia techniques – that brings to life *Tam o' Shanter*, one of Burns' best-loved poems.

www.burnsheritagepark.com
☎ 01292 443700—Open all year , daily

[P] [☕] [S] [WC]

24 Writers' Museum, Edinburgh

Lady Stair's House, Lawnmarket
The Writers' Museum occupies the historic Lady Stair's House, which was built in 1622.

The museum's Burns collection includes his writing desk, rare manuscripts, portraits, as well as many other mementoes. Other writers featured are Sir Walter Scott and Robert Louis Stevenson.

www.cac.org.uk
☎ 0131 529 4901—Open Mon-Sat all year 10.00-17.00; also open Sun 14.00-17.00 in Aug

[S] [WC]

Glossary

Aaboon	above	**dint**	occasion
agley	awry	**doup**	backside, bottom
a' tint	all lost		
ane anither	one another	**drouthy**	thirsty
asklent	obliquely	**duddies**	clothes
auld	old	**fand**	found
aye	always	**fash**	bother, trouble
beld	bald	**fere**	friend, companion
belvye	by-and-by		
bethankit	be thankful	**fit**	foot, foothold
bickerin' brattle	as if in a short race (in To a Mouse)	**flichterin**	fluttering
		flannen	flannel
billie	young man	**flit**	move
blellum	an idle-talking fellow	**fou**	full (or drunk)
		frae	from
bogles	ghosts, hobgoblins	**fyke**	fidget
		gane	gone
bousing	drinking	**gang**	go
brae	hill, or high ground by river	**gars**	make
		ghaists	ghosts
braid	broad	**gibbet-airns**	gibbet irons
brak's	broke his	**gie**	give
brent	smooth	**giglets**	giggling children
brithers	brothers		
burn	stream	**gin**	before
byke	bee-hive; swarm, crowd	**gowans**	flowers (daisy, dandelion, hawkweed)
cantie	cheerful		
cantraip	charm, spell	**gowd**	gold
carlin	old woman	**graith**	equipment, tools
chapman	pedlar		
clash	scandal, gossip	**gree**	social degree
cleekit	linked themselves	**greet**	weep
		gude-willie waught	generous drink
clew	past tense of to claw	**hain'd rig**	enclosed ridge (that is, safe place)
coost	cast		
cot	cottage	**hame**	home
countra clatter	country gossip	**heckle**	flax-comb
creeshie	greasy	**houghmagandie**	sexual love

houlets	owls
hurdies	hips, haunches
ingle	fireplace (wee bit ingle=small fireplace)
ithers	others
jaup	splash
keckle	laugh
kend	known
kennin	little bit
key-stane	keystone
kiaugh	anxiety
kytes	bellies
laith	loath
lang	long
lang syne	ancient (old times' sake)
loup	jump
luggies	wooden dish
mair	more
maun	must
mickle	much
mither	mother
monie, mony	many
nae	no
nappy	strong ale
nieve	fist
nit	nut
ony	any
paidl'd	paddled
plack	coin
pou'd	pulled, gathered
pow	poll (of head)
quean	young woman
raucle	rough, sturdy
rax	stretch
rigwoodie	withered, wizened
rung	cudgel
sae	so
sair	a) serve; b) sorry

sconner	loathe, disgust
sic	such
skellum	worthless fellow
skelpit	raced
skinking	watery
skreich	screech
sleekit	sleek, sly
sonsie	buxom, plump, good-natured
spean	wean
stacher	stagger
stane	stone
staw	to steal, or to surfeit
stoup	measure (of drink), tankard
taps	tops
tentie	careful
thairm	intestines
thegither	together
they lane	by yourself (literally, thy lone)
thrissle	thistle
tousie	shaggy
toyte	totter
tyke	vagrant dog
unco	very; odd
usquabea	whisky
walie	ample, large
weel	well
weel-swall'd	well-swollen
wha hae	who have
whins	furze-bush
wordy	worthy
wrang	wrong

Index